PRAISE FOR *THE LUCKY FEW*

A page turner. A hope giver. A life changer. Lucky are those who read these pages—their hearts will explode with the joy that we all truly get to be the luckiest of all.

ANN VOSKAMP, author of the *New York Times* bestsellers *The Broken Way* and *One Thousand Gifts*

I absolutely love this book. I love Heather Avis dearly, and her warmth and passion and fierce love come through on every page. This is a story about adoption, about family, about special needs . . . and really, more than anything, it's a story about faith. I'm so incredibly inspired by the way Heather listens to God's voice, and as I put down this book, I prayed for more of that kind of faith in my own life.

SHAUNA NIEQUIST, *New York Times* bestselling author of *Savor* and *Present Over Perfect*

If you've ever felt overwhelmed by the task before you, you will find a companion in this book. This book details the incredible adventure of the Avis family as they face some of life's greatest challenges and turn them into beautiful opportunities. It gives each of us hope in our own journey full of insurmountable odds.

DONALD MILLER, *New York Times* bestselling author of *Blue Like Jazz* and *Scary Close*

As a fellow Down syndrome mama, Heather Avis's words drew me in, igniting my heart from the very first page. Her powerful honesty and passion will light you aflame too, reminding us all that the path beyond easy and normal is the most precious. It's where we find God and become the lucky few.

REBEKAH LYONS, author of *Freefall to Fly*
and *You Are Free*

When I first met Heather Avis, I was drawn to her family's story because we share a love for foster care and adoption. But *The Lucky Few* is about so much more. Heather shows us what it means to seek after the heart of God, and she inspires us to do the same. You'll want to buy this book for everyone you know.

ANDY STANLEY, communicator,
author, and pastor

Heather is a modern-day superwoman with a heart that is brave and true. She doesn't pretend parenting is easy or that she hasn't faced darkness and been broken many times over. But she is honest. She chooses to risk every time. She chooses love, and even in the face of great struggle, she has said yes and jumped. Heather's face showed up for me the moment I was crumbling. I was scared for our daughter, and her words breathed hope into my trembling soul. This book will make your heart and arms open wide. It may cause your family to grow in numbers or move you to hold close the babies you have—plus ugly cry. It may cause all these things. This book is a testament to the power of a mother's love.

LISA GUNGOR, songwriter, musician, and
other half of musical collective Gungor

What started as a social hashtag has turned into a movement for the way we look at our lives. In *The Lucky Few*, Heather Avis shares a story that is honest, raw, hopeful, and deeply inspiring. May we all see the world—and its people—through this beautiful lens.

RACHEL HOLLIS, author and lifestyle expert at TheChicSite.com

Heather Avis is a guide for all of us "lucky few" walking in the wilderness. She reveals the exquisite beauty always hiding within the brokenness, the promise that in the darkness God is up to something bright and colorful. Joy is always waiting in the paths we would never choose for ourselves. As I read it, I felt like I was sitting with a good friend over coffee, letting her remind me all over again to notice God's grace right here in the middle of my own story.

MICHA BOYETT, author of *Found:*
A Story of Questions, Grace, and Everyday Prayer

With profound honesty, Heather Avis describes the bold journey she and Josh took into the world of Down syndrome and adoption—a journey where "joy and sorrow are so perfectly interwoven." *The Lucky Few* is filled with metaphors of hope: beauty shaped from the shards of broken dreams, stars of light bursting through darkness, fragile heartbeats filling the lonely silence. But beneath the hopeful metaphors are the hard, daily choices to trust God with life-threatening surgeries, with unexpected birth families, with overwhelming feelings of inadequacy, with moments when bravery feels remarkably like "wanting to puke." Though I intended to scan this book quickly, I found I had to read slowly, in part because the story was utterly captivating, but equally because God was using Heather's words to challenge me to be braver, to be more willing to step into the unknown, to be more prayerful and trusting.

LYNNE HYBELS, advocate for global engagement,
Willow Creek Community Church

This is a beautiful and honest story about coming to grips with God's best for your life—especially when society's expectations clash with your reality. God's grace in finding perfect children for Heather and Josh Avis and growing in them the courage to become the parents these children need is witness to all of us looking for divine clarity in the midst of seemingly confusing and sometimes devastating circumstances.

MARK REDDY, president of The JUSTICE Conference

The Lucky Few is a book about the deep-unto-deep kind of love we have as parents, a love with power over fear. Heather Avis's voice is a beaming light that infuses me with courage, not because she herself is braver than the rest of us, but because she shows us in this beautiful story that we must put down our expectations and ridiculous bootstrap mentalities so we can open ourselves to the intimate love God has for us. This book is a beacon for anyone who thinks she can't do the very thing she must.

AMBER C. HAINES, author of *Wild in the Hollow*

Heather Avis is an inspiration as a mom and as a woman. If I didn't know her personally, I would wonder if the grace pouring through her words was authentic. But she is the real deal, and her story of love makes me want to be a better mother and a better person.

LAURA TREMAINE, writer and podcaster

Oftentimes we see people do courageous acts, like adopt children with special needs, and we assume they are fearless heroes. Heather shows us that courage is actually birthed out of fear and disappointment. You will see yourself in her story and will be inspired to move through your own fears and disappointments in order to live a more courageous life.

JESSICA HONEGGER, founder of Noonday Collection

The Lucky Few is a beautiful and compelling story about the transformation of fear into hope. As you read about the Avis's journey, you'll be inspired to imitate their courageous surrender to the life-changing invitation of Jesus.

> MIKE ERRE, host of the VOXPodcast and team
> leader at VOX Christian Community

Heather Avis's words and story exemplify one of the hardest but most beautiful truths in motherhood—that you cannot predict the path on which it will lead you, but if you show up wholeheartedly, willing to be stretched by love, the greatest joy you've ever known is guaranteed to light the way. I'm inspired to stir up more areas of "comfortable noes" in my life and see, as Heather has beautifully shown us, how life expands into more grace and joy with a simple *yes*.

> KELLE HAMPTON, author of the *New York Times*
> bestselling memoir *Bloom*

Heather Avis's story is both exceptional and relatable. While the details may differ, many of us have found that life does not always go according to plan, and that sometimes we are placed on a path we never expected. Heather's book shares her personal journey with infertility, adoption, special needs parenting, and, ultimately, learning that our best-laid plans may be exchanged for something better than we could have ever imagined.

> KRISTEN HOWERTON, freelance writer
> and marriage and family therapist

The Lucky Few gives a glimpse into the remarkableness of one couple who choose a terrifying yes over an uncomfortable no—over and over again. It is an honest and vulnerable account of determination, not only to see God's promises come to pass, but also to seek his best for those whom society so often overlooks. Heather calls our attention to the image of God in every person and provides another lens through which to view the world and each person we encounter. By the end, you will see why the Avis family truly are the lucky few—and you just may end up wanting to join their crew as well!

VICKIE REDDY, executive producer of
The JUSTICE Conference

I so admire Heather Avis's tremendous faith and willingness to let God lead her. Her family's story will encourage so many other families just waiting to be brought together. This book will make you remember what true love looks like in action.

SARAH DUBBELDAM, editor-in-chief/
creative director of *Darling* magazine

the lucky few

Finding God's Best in the Most Unlikely Places

heather avis

ZONDERVAN®

ZONDERVAN

The Lucky Few
Copyright © 2017 by Heather Avis

Requests for information should be addressed to:
Zondervan, *3900 Sparks Dr. SE, Grand Rapids, Michigan 49546*

ISBN 978-0-310-34546-6 (softcover)

ISBN 978-0-310-34549-7 (ebook)

The names and details of some of the individuals depicted in this book have been changed to protect their privacy.

The author is represented by Alive Literary Agency, 7680 Goddard Street, Suite 200, Colorado Springs, Colorado 80920, www.aliveliteray.com.

Cover design: Micah Kandros
Cover photo: Sami Lane Photography http://samilane.com/
Interior design: Kait Lamphere

First Printing January 2017 / Printed in the United States of America

This book is for my wild flowers—
Macyn Hope, Truly Star, and August Ryker.
My luck began with you.

Contents

Foreword

More than a decade ago, God whispered to my heart that my husband and I were to adopt two boys from Liberia. *No*, I thought. *Not me.*

I felt like sticking my fingers in my ears and singing, *La, la, la, la, la . . . I'm not listening to You, God!* But the stirring in my soul wouldn't stop.

Doubts and questions flooded our minds: How could we financially increase the size of our family? How would we find the time in our already crammed schedule? How would we raise boys in our home of all girls? How would we find room? The list went on and on.

One day, I called my friend and poured out my heart. I told her I could list off many other parents who I felt were much more qualified than us. She patiently listened without much response as I asked, "Why me?"

Then quietly and prayerfully she answered: "Because God knew you'd say yes, Lysa."

I really believe with all my heart that God gave Josh and Heather the same kind of blessed assignment. Because he knew they'd say yes. Macy, Truly, and August—their beautiful adopted children (two of whom have Down Syndrome)—have made Josh and Heather exclaim with joy, "We are the lucky few."

I have been so inspired watching them parent and love their children like crazy. They consistently turn to God to gain a unique perspective—whether they are in a season of heartache or a season of celebration.

In these pages, Heather shares the raw realities of taking a journey that turned sharply away from comfortable down a path they never envisioned. I know just how terrifying that can be. But woven throughout her words is a truth we all need to hold close: some of God's greatest blessings burst forth from our greatest uncertainties.

This is more than just a book about adoption. This is a family love story pulsing with the very best kind of life.

Josh and Heather, I wholly agree. You are the lucky few. And what a joy it is to have a front-row seat to learn from you and cheer you on.

I have just one request. Those family dance parties y'all are always having? I get invited to the next one. Yes?

LYSA TERKEURST, *New York Times* bestselling
author and president of Proverbs 31 Ministries

Introduction

About a decade ago, when my husband and I decided the time had come to begin our family, I thought I knew what I wanted: a baby or two or three, born of my womb, bearing my eyes and his nose. Like every woman I've met, I wanted healthy children, because healthy seems easier; healthy seems normal; healthy seems nice.

What I did not know then is that ease and normalcy and niceness are not as important to Jesus as obedience, perseverance, and sacrifice. I didn't know then that easy and normal and nice would do little to build my character or make me a better and more complete human being.

Somewhere off the rose-petal path where easy, normal, and nice bloom, true beauty lives in the muck. But only the lucky few of us who step off the path will find it. My luck began when God picked me up off the comfortable path I had paved for myself and drop-kicked me into the mud.

In the beginning, all I wanted to see was the grime on my clothes and the dirt on my hands. But because of God's grace, I finally stopped looking for a way back to my own plans. And the farther I stepped from that pretty path of easy, normal, and nice, the more clearly I could see the beauty he was creating all around me. Far from my simple expectations of parenting, I discovered a richness and depth of life available to everyone.

I began to trust. In fact, I no longer needed to see beauty ahead of me in order to take a step toward it. I began to walk in the wilderness of God's love, and with each step, I watched his perfect will for my life unfold around me.

The three children Josh and I have the privilege of parenting today are not the ones I would have found on the path I had set out for myself. They are my wildflowers, pushing their way through the dirt and stretching up to the sun. My wildflowers have required me to be a certain kind of wild myself—the kind of wild I couldn't have become on my own. Today I can see I was created for profound experiences far beyond the reach of simple expectations.

So were you.

I look back on the past ten years, and there is little, if anything, I'd change about my journey. Every decision, celebration, and mistake have been pieced together in a map of grace that has led me to the life I have the honor of living today. But if I could, I would go back in time and talk to my twenty-four-year-old self. I would tell her to stop praying to get pregnant and to start asking God for a heart that beats like his. A heart that insists on beating to a rhythm other than God's can be a broken and aching heart indeed. It can be a painful process to change the rhythm of one's heart to match the rhythm of the heartbeat of God. A *lub-dub lub-dub* to a *ba-bum*. But I wouldn't trade the experience for anything else.

Even now as I write these words, I'm taken aback. These are the words, the truth, I need to be reminded of day after day. Because this is what I know: I have heard the Lord's heartbeat the loudest while walking in the wilderness, far from the easy path I stepped out on years ago.

this Was Not
the Plan

She's here!" I said to my husband, Josh, on the other end of the phone. I could hear music in the background and pictured him sitting on our white couch at home, his laptop beside him.

I was calling from a tiny hospital waiting room just outside the labor and delivery unit. Brightly colored chairs lined the stark white walls. Other than the muted TV flashing the day's most important news stories, I was alone.

"That was quick," Josh said. "Did you make it there for the birth?"

"Just barely. When Mom and I walked through the door, Harmony was ready to push. Ten minutes later, Kalli was born. It was surreal."

I brought my feet up onto the chair and rested my head on my knees. It was a beautiful spring evening, yet a chill came over me. I hugged my knees to my chest and began to shiver.

"Well, congratulations, Auntie!" Josh's joy was met with my silence. His voice got soft. "Are you okay?"

I felt the knot in my throat begin to grow as my eyes welled with tears. I sat there silently holding the phone with one hand, wiping away tears with the other.

"Babe, are you there?" he asked gently.

"Yes. I'm here," I said in a weepy whisper. "I'm just so sad. It should have been me. It was my turn. This is just not fair. I don't understand." And I let the floodgates open, my head on my knees, my phone drenched with tears.

"I'm so sorry. I am so, so sorry." Josh knew better than to try to fix this unfixable situation. If there was one thing he had learned about me during our years of infertility, it was that sometimes I just wanted to be sad. Sometimes the possible solutions he'd throw my way would make me want to scream and throw things.

"This is so sucky." I took a deep breath and tried to calm down. "I'm excited for my sister. I love my new niece so much already, but it was my turn." The tears started again. "It was my turn."

I always knew I would be a mom. As a child, when anyone asked, "What do you want to be when you grow up?" my answer was always, "A mom!"

I had a pretty ideal childhood. I grew up in a safe small town with my mom, dad, and two sisters. I grew up feeling safe, cared for, and loved. My mom stayed home and took care of us girls and the house and my dad. She is full to the brim with love and grace, and it overflows and drenches all who know her. As a child, I was constantly stepping in her puddles of grace. She made mothering look easy, and her ability to mother the way she did made me long for motherhood even more. My dream was to take all that love and grace I had soaked up and squeeze it out onto kids of my own.

By the time I entered college, I was dating Josh, a thoughtful and funny and darn good-looking artist. I had known him for years and knew he was the man I wanted to have babies with, the man I wanted to grow old with. I was twenty years old when we married, and I toasted my new husband with a champagne flute full of sparkling apple cider. Our wedding day was a dream, engulfed in God's goodness and favor.

I loved our first year of marriage. With one year of college left, we lived in a 650-square-foot apartment and waited for our financial-aid checks to come in the mail so we could pay rent and buy groceries.

Between classes and homework, Josh worked as a valet-parking atten-
dant. We kept his tips in a jar on the fridge, reaching for dollar bills
to fill up our gas tanks and our cupboards. He usually parked cars
at fancy restaurants, and from time to time, he would come home
with takeout containers full of food we could never afford to buy.
I would set our tiny table for two—the one crammed against the
wall overlooking the parking lot of our apartment complex. I'd light
a candle, and we would sit at our tiny table, indulging in expensive
food and making plans for a big, adventurous future, which began as
soon as we graduated.

We took a six-month detour to the island of Maui before ending up
in the quaint Southern California city of Redlands. There I took a job
as a special-education teacher while I pursued my teaching credentials,
and Josh began working as a graphic designer. Life was good. It was
easy. Comfortable.

My older sister, Harmony, called me while I was at work one morning.
I let the call go to voice mail, and her vague "hi, it's me; call me back
as soon as you can" led me to call her just as soon as the bell rang for
my students to take a break. I shooed them out the door and locked it
so I could make the call with no interruptions.

"Hey, Harm. What's going on?"

"Heather, you're going to be an auntie!" She yelled so loudly I had
to pull the phone away from my ear.

"What? No way? Oh my gosh, Harmony! This is so exciting!" I was
jumping up and down and shouting with joy. Some of my students
gathered around my locked door, knocking to get in and see what all
the commotion was about.

I motioned for them to go away. "The bell to come in has not rung yet!" I yelled through the crack in the door.

"Sorry about that. I can't even believe it. How are you feeling? When are you due?" I had a smile plastered to my face.

"I'm super pukey but really excited. I'm due at the end of June. Heath, you have to come up for the birth," Harmony said.

"Of course! I wouldn't miss it for the world."

The bell for class rang, and my students began banging on the locked door.

"Hold your horses, kiddos!"

Harmony, having been a teacher herself, knew my time was limited. "I'll let you go. Bye, Auntie Heather." Her voice was full of smiles.

"Bye, Mama!" I hung up the phone, the love for my soon-to-be niece or nephew already beginning to grow.

Nine months later, I got the call that Harmony had gone into labor. Our mom and I drove to the airport and jumped on the first available flight to get to where she lived in Northern California. I sat in the labor and delivery room, feeding Harmony ice chips and holding her leg as she pushed her son into the world.

When Jaxon was a few months old, Josh and I drove to Harmony's home so he could meet his new nephew. I remember sitting on Harmony's extra-cushy tan couch with Jaxon cradled on my legs, his head on my knees, his feet gently kicking my belly.

"Gosh, Harm, could you have created a more adorable child?" I said. Jaxon smiled up at me with his perfectly round head and massive cheeks.

"He's pretty cute," Harmony yelled out from the kitchen. The scents of fresh basil and sweet tomatoes were filling the house. Seeing Harmony as a mom made me want to be one even more.

Jaxon blew raspberries as he continued to smile up at me. "Harm,

I think we should get pregnant at the same time for your next baby. How fun would that be?"

Harmony came out, wiping her hands on a kitchen towel. "I was already planning on it."

She sat next to me on the couch, and Jaxon's face beamed when he saw his mama. "We'll have a joint baby shower," she said. "It'll be a blast." She scooped up Jaxon from my lap, and he spit up all over her shirt. "But can we wait a couple of years?"

"Oh, yes." I grabbed the kitchen towel from her hands and began wiping up the mess.

"At least a couple of years," Josh chimed in from his seat across the room.

A couple of years passed, and Josh and I decided it was time to grow our family. By then we were established in real adult careers that paid us salaries and provided us with medical insurance. So Josh and I took the steps needed to get pregnant. Because I was a teacher, we thought the best plan was one that aimed for a birthday near the summer months.

The counting game began. We would try to get pregnant at the optimal time, and I'd count the nine months to figure out when the baby would be born. Then I'd start my period—with grand disappointment—and the whole process would repeat the next month.

This cycle went on for months, each month becoming more painful than the last. A new school year started, one I had hoped to miss—at home with my baby.

About a month before that school year came to an end, I was sitting at my desk grading papers during my planning period when I heard an unexpected knock on my door.

My classroom was in a portable unit located at the far end of the school. I almost always left my classroom door open, but this day was particularly hot and the AC was pumping. I got up from my desk stacked with papers, notebooks, and folders and opened the door.

"Hey, Mrs. A. Do you have a minute?" It was one of my sophomore algebra students, Jen.

"Of course. Except, where are you supposed to be right now?"

She handed me a green slip. "I got this pass from Mrs. Frances. I told her I needed to go to the nurse, but really I just need someone to talk to." Her eyes were red and swollen, and her thick mascara had left a black map on her cheeks.

Jen and I had been through a lot that year. She stepped foot in my classroom the first day of school ready for a fight, doing everything she could to prove she was not worth loving. I liked her from the second we met. She was unaware that her type is my favorite type, and that I had patience for her shenanigans and could see right through the sharp exterior she had built to protect herself from life's circumstances. It took a couple of months, but she soon began to see in herself the potential I saw. She started to trust that an adult could have her best in mind.

"Well, come in, sweetie. Let's sit over here." We walked to the old blue couch pushed up against the window. I sat down on one end, and Jen collapsed right next to me and fell into my arms crying.

"Hey, Jen, what's going on?"

"I didn't think it could happen." She wiped her nose with the sleeve of her black lace sweater. "I mean, I had an abortion last year and thought I couldn't get pregnant again."

Dear, sweet Jesus, who is teaching these kids about the birds and the bees? "Honey, are you pregnant right now?"

"Mm-hmm." She nodded and began to sob. "My parents are going to kill me. I don't know what to do."

My heart sank. My heart sank so deep I didn't know if I would ever be able to retrieve it. My fifteen-year-old student with little to no support system was pregnant for the second time in a year. I sat in disbelief as she soaked my shoulder with her tears.

"Oh, honey, it's going to be okay. I can walk with you through this. I can be with you when you talk to your parents. It's going to be okay." While I comforted her, I felt the strangest mix of emotions. Sadness and jealousy begin to wrap themselves around every cell in my being and I, too, began to sob. We sat there together in the coolness of my classroom on my old blue couch. With eyes full of tears, I looked up to heaven. *This cannot be happening. Dear Jesus, what on earth?*

It seemed as though the situation with my student, Jen, marked the beginning of a frustrating, heartbreaking tornado of infertility. The history books may not reflect it, but in the years 2005–2008, everyone was having a baby. Everyone but me.

On Sunday mornings at church, I would look around in disbelief at the number of swollen bellies in the seats around me. One week, an associate pastor made a joke during announcements, saying there must be something in the water because so many women were expecting babies. I wanted to run up on the stage, punch him in the face, and then grab the mic and yell at everyone for being so insensitive and forgetting about me. But I sat in my seat with my fists clenched and my eyes welling with tears. Neither the pastor nor the women around me with glowing skin and maternity clothes were trying to hurt me, and I knew that. But the longing I felt for a baby was becoming more than I could bear. And really, there *must* have been something in the water.

"Heather, where are my new shorts?" Josh yelled from the laundry room.

"If they aren't in the dryer, I don't know," I called back.

The summer weather was calling for shorts and light dresses. I walked to the other side of the bed in our room and pulled the corner of the quilt straight. The windows were open, letting in the sound of the chirping birds and a wonderful summer breeze. Josh and I were about to embark on a rare, do-nothing kind of day. The phone rang.

I called to Josh, "Can you get that?" I heard him pick up the phone.

"Hey, Harmony," I heard him say. "Yeah, hang on, I'll get her." Josh walked in and handed me the phone. "It's your sister."

"Hey, Harm. What's up?"

"Well, guess what?" Her voice was a mix of hesitation and elation.

I knew. My stomach dropped. And panic set in because I didn't know how to respond and I didn't want to hear what she was going to say next. So I held the phone, silent.

"You're going to be an auntie again, Heather. I'm pregnant." Harmony made the announcement gently this time, knowing the pain it could cause. She had walked this brutal infertility path with me. She knew how desperate I was to be the one making that very announcement. She knew the plan we had made sitting in her living room. Together. We were supposed to have our babies together.

"Wow, Harmony. Congratulations." I began to pace the floor, trying so hard not to cry, but there was no stopping the tears.

"I'm sorry, Heath," Harmony whispered, she herself crying on the other end of the phone.

I took a deep breath, shoving my emotions aside so I could celebrate with my sister. I sat down on the freshly made bed, wrinkling the quilt.

"Harmony, do *not* be sorry. I am really and truly so happy for you guys. And I'm going to be an auntie again! You know how much I love being an auntie." Somehow I was able to stop my crying, take the focus off myself, and transfer it to where it belonged.

We talked for a few more minutes about due dates and morning sickness, and then I pushed the red button to hang up the phone and let it fall to the floor. Josh came and sat next to me on the bed, his arm around my shoulder. I buried my head in my hands and in complete and total brokenness wept, the sound of my sobs clashing with the song of the birds. Beauty and pain.

The phone call from Harmony was the rancid icing on the stale cake. My plans had officially fallen apart. It seemed as though God had pulled out the rug from under me, allowing me to tumble into this deep unknown, arms flailing, out of control. Little did I know that God was not only allowing it, but he was ushering me there, into the depths of *his* plans.

So I fell. Brokenhearted and gasping for air, I grabbed hold of anything I could to help me fill my belly with a baby. Out of the kindness of their hearts, people told me to relax more, to eat this, to not eat that, to get away for the weekend, to stop thinking about it, to go shopping for new clothes. Out of desperation, I tried it all. But the thing is, friends, a relaxing weekend in Palm Springs noshing on organic kale and buying a new wardrobe will not get a girl pregnant.

So I ended up in the office of a fertility specialist. His price tag was high, but money is just money to a desperate person. I answered questions and sat through an exam. Discoveries led me weeks later into a different doctor's office and then onto an operating table for a diagnostic surgery. More weeks passed, and I found myself undergoing an invasive and painful dye test, which led to a terrible and freakish infection, which resulted in several visits to the ER.

When I was well enough to go back to work, I made an appointment with my ob-gyn to figure out what had happened and what the next step would be.

I arrived for my appointment a few minutes early. The waiting area was hopping. I found an empty seat next to an expectant mom who looked about ready to pop. I kept my head down, afraid I'd accidently give her a dirty and jealous look. This infertility business was a nasty thing. I grabbed the closest magazine and mindlessly flipped through the pages, looking at photos of babies and moms, skimming the "Top 10 Toys" and parenting how-tos.

"Heather." At the sound of my name, I tossed the useless magazine on my chair. "It's nice to see you again," the nurse said, and I followed her over to the scale. She took my weight and led me across the hall.

"The doctor will see you in his office today, right over here."

I thought it was strange we would meet there rather than in an exam room. We had always met in an exam room.

"Have a seat. He'll be right in." She closed the door and walked away.

I sat in the overstuffed chair across from my doctor's cluttered desk. Behind it were floor-to-ceiling bookshelves full of medical journals and framed pictures of his family. His wife looked young, sandwiched between him and his two daughters. Seeing the photo of his family made me wonder if they had any trouble conceiving. Could he relate to his patients at all?

My thoughts were interrupted by a soft knock at the door and then the creaking of the hinges as my doctor stepped into his office.

"Heather, what in the world happened?" His Eastern European accent was thick.

"Well, that's what I'm here to find out. What *did* happen?"

"First, I am sorry about the timing of things. That I was out of town when you were in and out of the emergency room. I've read your chart, but please do tell me in your own words what happened after the dye test."

He sat behind the desk.

"Well, a couple of days after, I was at home having dinner with friends when I started feeling some awful cramping. Within a couple of hours, I was in a fetal position on the floor, in unbelievable amounts of pain. My husband took me to the emergency room, and for more than a week, I was in and out of the ER, in unspeakable pain. The doctor on call told me the dye test had led to a terrible infection in my reproductive organs. He gave me antibiotics. Honestly, the whole thing is a bit of a blur. I still don't feel 100 percent." The tone of my voice was matter-of-fact and almost accusatory.

"Again, I'm sorry this happened to you. Less than 2 percent of women who have the dye test are prone to an infection of that magnitude."

"So, what does this mean for me?" As soon as I asked the question, I had a feeling I did not want to know the answer. I looked at the door and thought about running. But it was too late; he was already talking.

I watched his mouth move, his brow furrow, and his head shake in pity, but I was having an out-of-the-body experience. The world around me began spinning and only select words out of his mouth— "permanent damage," "inability to bear children," "nothing we can do"—came into focus, like big neon signs flashing the doom of my future. I stared out the window at the beautiful, sunny Southern California day while he said in so many words that I am infertile, that without lots of invasive and unnatural assistance from specialists in the field, there is simply no way my body can do its part in making a baby.

"Heather? Are you okay?" His voice brought me back to reality.

"Uh-huh." It was the only sound I could make.

"Can I answer any questions?"

"Nuh-uh." I knew if I began to speak, I would crumble into a million broken pieces right there on his office floor.

"Okay, well I want to see you back in a month for a full exam. Again, I am so sorry all of this happened to you." His eyes reflected his sincerity.

I gave a weak smile and bolted for the door. I walked as quickly as I could through the crowded waiting room, pushing my way through the sea of pregnant women. I ran down the stairwell to the ground floor and out the automatic double doors and gasped for air.

There were people all around me. Some were on their phones. One was in a wheelchair. I didn't really see any of them, but I know they had to have seen me. I know they saw me, because I was the woman on the sidewalk, unashamedly sobbing. The news struck deep into the core of me, killing who I thought I was or needed to be, slowly, and painfully severing my womanhood from my being.

As I walked toward my car, broken and weeping, I let go of the hope I had clung to like the string of a balloon. Sadness consumed me as all the hope I had left floated away. This thing—a woman's ability to create and grow children—did not exist in me. There was nothing I could do about it. There was no new plan I could put into place so I could gain control over what should be a natural aspect of womanhood. All my womanly parts were there, but they were broken, and unlike a car that refuses to get from point A to point B, replacing or fixing the broken pieces was not an option.

The news I received that afternoon is life-altering news, the kind that cannot be taken back, the kind that enters through your ears and into your brain and somehow seeps into every drop of blood pulsating through your body. When I got home, I made my way to my room and collapsed onto my bed. I sank into the mattress, hyperaware of my empty womb and the string of hope I had let slip through my fingers. I felt numb, wishing for yesterday to come find and rescue me. Yesterday was full of plans and possible solutions, and false ideas about what I could control. Yesterday I had hope of a working womb, one ready and excited to grow a life and make me a mom.

The book of Isaiah tells of a God who gives us "a crown of beauty instead of ashes, the oil of joy instead of mourning, and a garment of praise instead of a spirit of despair" (61:3). That day after my appointment, I woke up with no new plans to fix my problems and gain control of my situation. I felt like a pile of ashes, my purpose and abilities consumed by a fire. And like a pile of ashes being blown in the wind, my hope for becoming a mother swirled around me, a dirty mess.

But God's Word whispered in my ear, "There is beauty here . . . yes even here."

First Light

As a kid, I loved to poke holes in sheets of black paper. I would sit on the carpet and use a sharp pencil to make a thoughtless, almost violent mess. But then I'd take the ugly paper and hold it up to a light, creating a beautiful piece of artwork.

In our season of infertility, that is how I felt God was working on me. All I could see before me was a dark and messy situation. I stared at it day in and day out. I allowed the darkness to grow around me until it was all I could see in every direction. Then God used his super-sharp pencil to puncture my darkness. In the pain of that puncture, a glimmer of hope began to shine on me.

For a few weeks after learning the loss of my fertility would be permanent, my husband and I had conversations about adoption. We would sit at the computer, educating ourselves about the different possibilities. With each conversation Josh and I had, God would take his pencil and poke another hole into the darkness I had let consume me.

At the time we started to consider adoption seriously, we did not know one person who had taken that path to parenthood. We didn't know where to begin or what to ask or whom to ask. But as God kept poking holes of glorious light into my emotional walls, we found out one of my coworkers had two adopted grandsons. She put us in touch with her son and daughter-in-law, and we set a date for dinner.

"That's the house, there on the left." I pointed to the average-size, ranch-style house with the manicured lawn. Josh parked on the curb across the street. I got out of the passenger seat and walked around to the other side of the car. We stood side by side just looking at the house.

Josh grabbed my hand, gave it a squeeze, and said, "Are you ready for this?"

"As I'll ever be."

We crossed the street, walked up the paved path, and rang the doorbell. From behind the closed door, we heard little feet running and loud voices, and then the door swung open.

"Hey! You must be Josh and Heather. I'm Don." The man who opened the door, my coworker's son, radiated joy. His six-foot-six frame and firefighter build had the potential to be intimidating, but the spirit that shone through his eyes and smile was anything but. He reached out, shook Josh's hand, and then pulled me in for a bear hug.

"Welcome to our home. Please come on in." We followed him through a comfy living space toward the kitchen. The house was welcoming and tidy except for a random foam sword and scattered Legos, evidence of their sons. "This is my wife, Diana."

"Hey, guys. Welcome. I'm so glad this worked out." Diana had short blond hair and a kind and radiant smile like her husband's. Her bright, blue eyes offered understanding and put me at ease. Immediately Josh and I felt at home in this place.

"Thank you so much for having us." Josh's response was interrupted by the sound of yelling and pounding feet headed in our direction.

"Whoa, whoa, boys! Slow it down," Diana called out as Don scooped up the littlest one.

"Say hi to our new friends," Don said.

The boys gave a heartfelt hello in unison as the littlest one wiggled out of his dad's arms, and then they were on their way.

"Boys are crazy." Diana's eyes twinkled. "But oh so fun."

Their eldest son, Nathan, was tall and lanky, with big brown eyes and light brown skin, and I'd swear he looked just like his dad. Their younger son, Roman, was small for his age, with fair skin and blond hair, and I'd swear he looked just like his mom.

We sat down at the round table in the dining room. They had picked up a feast from a local barbecue joint, and we all piled our plates full of tangy and sticky grilled chicken, fall-off-the-bone ribs, and buttery corn on the cob.

"My mom tells me y'all want to adopt," Don said.

"We really do. We just have no idea where to start." I licked barbecue sauce off my thumb.

"Well, we're happy to share our boys' stories with you and answer your questions," Diana said as she leaned over her youngest son's plate, cutting meat into bite-size pieces.

"Is it okay to talk about this in front of the boys?" I felt uncomfortable, not knowing how much their boys knew about where they came from. I didn't want to ask the wrong questions and open up a wound—or worse.

"Of course," Don said. "Our boys know exactly who they are. We talk about adoption openly and celebrate how our family came to be. We believe it's best to make adoption part of their story from the beginning. It's our normal."

"Yup," Diana agreed. "No secrets or surprises."

"Okay, that makes sense." I loved their approach. "So tell us how your boys became your boys."

We spent the next hour or so learning their sons' adoption stories. We discovered that when adopting through a private agency, as these new friends of ours did, some kind of relationship with the birth parent is likely. Their boys received pictures and letters once a year. Some people who adopt have wide-open relationships with their children's birth parents, meeting in person once a year or more. Don and Diana told us the cost of a private adoption could be $20,000 or more. The agency they used was one of the most affordable.

As we asked questions and chatted, I watched this family interact like just that—a family. They were not unusual or awkward. The boys didn't seem to care that they didn't share DNA with their parents or each other. Don and Diana are their mom and dad, and Nathan and Roman are each other's brother. We sat in their home and quickly realized that genes can have nothing to do with what makes a family.

This home made up of people who each came from a different woman's womb was divine and, well, normal. They were a genuine and lovely family, typical as can be. It was apparent to us that God's good and perfect will covered them with a divine netting of love and desires and needs and calling and life. And this man and woman, this mom and dad, were happily tangled up in this beautiful and mysterious web.

After hours of eating and talking and asking questions and witnessing the divine, it was time for Josh and me to go. For weeks, I had been flailing in darkness, my wounds from the news still fresh and tender. But as our new friends walked us to the door and sent us off with big bear hugs—Diana holding Roman on her hip, Don's arm resting on Nathan's shoulders—my heart began to lighten a bit.

The door closed, and we turned toward our car. I gave Josh's hand a tight squeeze. We stood on their front porch for a moment, silent, taking in all we had just witnessed.

Josh broke the silence. "What a great family."

"Yeah. They seem so normal. I loved that."

"So, what do you think? What's next?" Josh let go of my hand and put his arm around me as we walked toward the car.

I wavered. Adoption is risky, with more unknowns than knowns.

Even though what we had witnessed was great, I knew adoption meant letting go of all my ideas about how motherhood would find me. I knew I would have to be open to a child born into brokenness. I figured the path ahead would be slippery and dangerous. Yet I kept hearing God whisper to me, "There is beauty ahead. Yes, beauty in this unknown."

So as we walked to our car that night, Josh and I held on tightly to each other and set our feet firmly on the path of adoption.

A year later, in the summer of 2008, I found myself in a small motel room in Romania sitting at my computer and reading an e-mail that would change everything.

Ten days earlier, Josh and I had landed in this beautiful country with a group of people to do a summer camp for youth in the Carpathian Mountains. We had spent a week pouring ourselves into these young world changers, sharing our hearts and falling in love with theirs. The camp we stayed at was in the middle of nowhere, way up in the mountains. Getting there required hours in a stuffy bus, driving over pothole-stricken roads with hairpin turns. But the destination was breathtaking.

We were surrounded by fields and forests so green and lush I wanted to make a quilt from their splendor, pack it in my suitcase, and take it home to enjoy forever. Though it was the middle of a hot summer, nights in the Carpathian Mountains were close to freezing. The camp offered warm feather beds and down comforters, which we wrapped ourselves in as we lay in the grass and looked up at the stars. Oh those stars! I had never seen anything like it. In parts of the sky, the stars were so crowded that there was more light than darkness. I would look up at those stars, breathless and in awe, and thank God he was using this time in these mountains with these youths to crowd out the darkness in my life.

I love that when God pokes holes in our darkness to let in his glorious light, he doesn't stop until the brilliance overtakes the black. As I stared at those stars over Romania, I couldn't believe I'd been hoping we'd be somewhere else.

Before making the trip to this beautiful country, our third time here, Josh and I had selected a private adoption agency and were placed on a list of families waiting to adopt. We created a profile with pictures of us smiling and traveling, vacationing, and spending time with friends and extended family. Our presentation was being viewed by mothers creating an adoption plan for the children in their wombs. As we prepared to leave for Romania, a large piece of my heart was hoping our trip would be interrupted by a phone call from our social worker letting us know we'd been chosen. I had prayed that rather than hop onto an airplane, we'd hop into our car and drive to meet the baby we had been longing for all these years.

By the time we left, I accepted the fact that I would have empty arms and a longing heart and a love for an unknown baby for at least a few more weeks. After packing my bags, I sat down at my computer and typed a short note to our social worker.

Dear Lindsey,

I hope this e-mail finds you well. While I'm not expecting anything to happen, I just wanted to let you know that we will be out of the country from July 23–August 7. We will be checking our e-mail a couple of times and may have access to our voice mail as well if you need to reach us for any reason.

Thanks so much,

Heather

And that was that. The next day, we were on a plane, my arms full of suitcases and passports but my mind still full of thoughts about our future child.

When our time in the mountains came to an end, we made our way to a small motel in the city of Cluj-Napoca. The motel was old and worn, and the smell of stale cigarette smoke seeped from the floors and walls. But it was clean and safe, and we were on a budget. When we arrived, everyone in our group was famished, so we made plans to walk to a restaurant up the street.

"I have to run up to our room and grab a sweater," I said. Others needed to do the same, so we agreed to meet in front of the motel in ten minutes.

I ran up three flights of stairs to our less-than-luxurious room at the end of the hall.

As I opened the door, I caught myself humming. My heart was full to the brim with all that our experience in this lovely country had to offer. I found myself grateful I was there, in fact, and not waiting in my house for a phone call from our social worker.

I grabbed the gray sweater on the bed and noticed Josh's laptop sitting there. I looked at the clock on the wall and decided to check e-mail. Then I knelt on the floor next to the bed and opened the computer.

As I scanned my inbox, I saw the name of our social worker, and my heart skipped a beat. For a brief moment, I thought, *This could be the e-mail*, and then I remembered she was probably only replying to the message I'd sent before we left.

Before opening her message, I looked around the room, maybe to be sure I was alone or perhaps in hopes of finding out I wasn't. Something in the gut of my gut knew there was more to it. I clicked on the little icon of an envelope, and my life changed forever.

Dear Heather,

Thank you for the update. I hope you have a nice time. Just wanted you to know that your profile has been shown once. Things have been slow. We have recently had a few babies with Down syndrome placed with us, so finding homes for them is a little more difficult.

Hang in there.

Lindsey

My heart began to pound so loudly that the sound seemed to come from outside. On the surface, this short reply seemed meaningless, but it wasn't. I knew it. I just knew it.

I read the e-mail again. My mind told me to just shut the computer and say, "That's nice," and head downstairs for a fun-filled dinner. But my heart held on tightly to the words *a few babies with Down syndrome.* I found myself foolishly begin to argue with my heart. *I never wanted a child with Down syndrome,* I reminded it. That was not the plan. We were paying the big bucks for this adoption in hopes of getting a healthy child.

But as my heart beat in my chest I could not shake the words I had just read:

. . . a few babies with Down syndrome . . .

. . . babies with Down syndrome . . .

. . . Down syndrome . . .

I knew God was at work, and I was so disappointed.

I slammed the laptop closed and said out loud, "Dear Lord, what are you doing? Please don't change my heart. This is not in my plans."

I walked downstairs to the lobby. My head was spinning. For a moment, I blamed my dizziness on the odors of cigarette smoke mixing with the smells of foreign foods coming from the kitchen. Everyone was ready and had been waiting for me. I felt envious of the fact that their lives were the same now as they had been fifteen minutes ago. I wanted that to be the case for me, but already I knew that the life I was living fifteen minutes ago was a thing of the past.

I faked cool, calm, and collected. "Sorry about that. I'm ready. Let's go."

Josh saw through me. He grabbed my hand, and as the others moved up the street, he asked quietly, "You okay?"

I gave him a "what in the world could you mean?" kind of look. But when there was enough distance between us and the group I said, "I got an e-mail from Lindsey."

His blue eyes lit up. "Does she have a baby for us?"

"Not exactly."

"What's that mean?"

"Well, she said there are babies needing homes, but they have Down syndrome." The words sounded so foreign coming from my lips that I may as well have been speaking Romanian.

He met this piece of information with silence. Honestly, I wanted Josh to tell me there was no way we were going to adopt a baby with Down syndrome. I wanted him to take the lead here, and I wanted him to lead us far away from this.

"Wow! Okay. Well, what do *you* think?" Not the response I was hoping for. I tried again.

"I think it's crazy. What do *you* think?"

"I think we need to pray about it." He looked me square in the eyes and said, "And I think crazy is how we roll."

Oh, dear Lord, what are you up to now?

The next day we left Romania. We tearfully said our good-byes to the young people we had camped with in the mountains, our hearts now tied to theirs. As I said good-bye and told them I would do my best to return the following summer, I thought about the babies back home, the babies with Down syndrome who had so suddenly disrupted my life. I wondered if one of them would like this country as much as I did. Then I quickly changed my thoughts and told my heart to stop being so foolish. Why make plans for the future with a child we never intended to adopt?

After our time in Romania came to a close, Josh and I spent another week together in Europe. The next week we found ourselves getting from one destination to the next via small planes, city buses, fast trains, bumpy boat rides, wild taxicabs, and rickety bikes. We ended up on a tiny Greek island called Agistri. It was the kind of place that took some getting used to, like that perfect pair of shoes: a little awkward and uncomfortable at first, but soon you slide right in and never want to take them off.

While on this cozy and interesting island, we found ourselves walking on deserted beaches and crowded sidewalks, sipping cloudy and chilled ouzo at street-side café tables, and dining in lively restaurants. We ate fresh octopus that we had watched the fishermen bring in off the boat only minutes earlier. We feasted on plates overflowing with hummus, salty olives, fresh fish, and crisp cucumbers. We indulged in huge bowls of thick and tart Greek yogurt drowning in local honey. And during all these times, we found ourselves talking about just one thing: adopting a baby with Down syndrome.

"Okay," Josh would start as he reached for a pen from the backpack. "Pros and cons."

"Pros and cons? You seriously think we will make this decision with a pros and cons list?" I raised my eyebrows, full of sass. "We are talking about a child, not a new car."

"Don't look at me like that," he sassed right back. "I know what's at stake here. Pros and cons is a perfectly good way to help us make this decision."

"Okay. Pro: they're babies."

Josh wrote it on the pro side of the napkin as our waiter set a whole roasted fish, eyes and all, in front of me.

"Con: they have Down syndrome."

I cut off a piece of my fish and slathered it in hummus. Our meal continued this way. As we added to the list, the cons side grew and grew, far outnumbering the pros.

Now that we're on the other side of our decision, I look back on this time and cringe. I almost weep tears of sorrow and terror at the thought that we might have said no to our Macy girl. I get angry, understanding that we had let our culture taint us into thinking that Down syndrome should go on the cons list when it should have been one of our pros. Friends, Down syndrome is only ever a pro.

Down syndrome (also called Trisomy 21) occurs when a person is born with a third copy of the twenty-first chromosome. That's it. Doesn't seem like a big deal, right? This extra chromosome is responsible for some of the characteristics that are common among people with Down syndrome, including low muscle tone, small stature, an upward slant to the eyes, and a flat nasal bridge. In addition, people with Trisomy 21 have an increased risk for certain medical conditions, including thyroid conditions, congenital heart defects, respiratory and hearing problems, and Alzheimer's disease. These characteristics appear to varying degrees, sometimes not at all. It's extremely important to note that every person with Down syndrome is a unique individual. Most babies and young children require early intervention in the form of occupational therapy (to strengthen fine-motor and eating skills), physical therapy (to strengthen gross-motor skills), and speech therapy.

Most of humanity reads such a list and concludes that Down syndrome is a bad thing, as I was tempted to do when considering whether to adopt our first child. It's not "normal," it's not familiar; it's uncomfortable. This conclusion is most often made by those who have limited or no connection to an actual living, breathing person with Down syndrome. This is a problem. In my experience, those who take the time to develop such relationships quickly realize that Down syndrome is nothing to be afraid of. Many individuals who have Down syndrome are attending and graduating from college, living independently, and pursuing full-time careers. People with Trisomy 21 and those of us who love them are speaking up more and more about their beauty, abilities, and personhood.

Today I'm aware of all the times I have said no to opportunities God has placed before me because I think I'm not rich enough, equipped enough, talented enough, strong enough, or crazy enough to say yes. All the times I have mistaken good things for bad. All the times I have allowed the opinions of an ignorant majority to guide my thinking instead of looking to Jesus and his heart in the matter. I wonder how many times we, his children, choose a comfortable no over a terrifying yes—the kind of yes that will lead us to the only place we should ever long to be: in the arms of Jesus.

So there Josh and I were, sitting on the beaches of Greece and trying to come up with one good reason to say no to adopting a little baby with Down syndrome.

After our meal, we went down to the water and skipped smooth stones across the calm sea. The gentle waves lapped at our feet.

"I know the cons list is long," I said, "but is there one really good reason on that list? I mean *really* good?"

"Honestly, there isn't. Every con seems to be based on fear or ignorance."

"Right! And they're only cons if Jesus isn't in our picture. When I think from a worldly standpoint about adopting a child with Down syndrome, no is a perfectly reasonable answer. But when Jesus enters, that just doesn't seem like an option. Still, a yes answer seems crazy!"

"And really," Josh said, "when all is said and done, a baby is just a baby who needs a mom and dad. We can be that."

That's what it really came down to for us: in our hearts, we knew a baby with Down syndrome is a baby fearfully and wonderfully made. A baby in need of a family. A baby who wants to eat and sleep and snuggle. And while the world was telling us all the reasons we shouldn't adopt such a baby, God was working in our hearts, whispering softly and gently, reminding us that he is greater than any one of those items on the cons list. He was showing us we needed to trust him and also trust the instinct he had placed in our hearts. He was showing us not only a baby in need of a family, but the fact that we were a family in need of a baby.

"Argh!" I shouted. "This *is* crazy! People are going to think we're nuts if we step toward this."

"So let 'em think it. It's not far from the truth." Josh put his arm around me and pulled me close.

Our time in Greece came to an end, and we wheeled our heavy suitcases onto the train in Athens, heading to the airport for our long flight back to our little home in California. Standing there in the crowd of people, the reality of life and the decision sitting in our laps became very, very heavy.

I looked at Josh and said, "So, what now? What are we going to do when we get home?" I knew the answer before asking the question. Our new life was already in motion.

"We make a call. We take a step." Josh's response sounded practical and stale.

Honestly, both of us wished it could be something else. We wished the e-mail had never been sent, the conversations never taken place.

We found ourselves holding an uncomfortable responsibility. The only thing we knew for sure, for sure, for sure, was that God is good. But in this particular situation, I began to wonder if that would be enough.

The train came to a stop. We stepped off and entered the airport. Our adventures in Europe were coming to a close, but we knew a larger adventure, grander than any European escapade, was waiting for us on the other side of the globe.

We were excited. And terrified.

A Scary Yes

The morning after we got home, I jumped out of bed, eager to get our social worker on the phone. I took a deep breath and with clammy hands dialed the number.

"Hi, Lindsey, we just got home from our trip, and I wanted to talk to you about the babies with Down syndrome you mentioned in your e-mail." Josh and I sat on our couch together, the phone on speaker, a healthy kind of crazy gleam in our eyes.

"There were two. One of the babies was just matched with a family. It's too bad I didn't know you were interested; you would have been a great match for this little girl."

"How about the other baby?" Josh and I held our breath.

"Well, we just found out she has some serious health issues. She's actually scheduled for a heart procedure in a few days. We don't know what her prognosis is, so at this time we're not looking for a placement."

I felt like I had been sucker punched. "What exactly does that mean? Is she not adoptable?"

"Not right now. We'd like to see how she responds to this surgery. We want to know the extent of her medical needs before we put her in adoptive placement. Are you open to a child with Down syndrome?"

"Yes, I think we are."

"Okay, good to know. I'll change the information on your profile." If she was anything, she was matter-of-fact. "And hang in there, these things take time. You'll get your baby."

"I know. Thank you for the information."

I hung up the phone feeling greatly disappointed.

"What the heck?" Josh said.

"That was an awful lot of prayer and questioning and willingness to take a risk to end up here with no baby! I'm confused."

Josh tried to make sense of the situation. "Maybe God just wanted us to be open to any kind of baby?"

"I guess. And I'm so excited to see who that baby is. But what if we *don't* get a baby with Down syndrome?"

We sat there on the couch staring at each other, shocked by the words I had just spoken. Only days ago, we were shaking our heads at God for even suggesting we consider a child with Down syndrome. It was obvious to both of us that something much bigger than us was happening here. God was at work in a mystical and powerful way. But what in the world was he doing? What was he asking us to do?

Two months passed, and we stopped talking about a baby with Down syndrome, though we never forgot. We moved on in our minds and in our actions. Life went on, as it had since we began the adoption process. Josh and I had full-time jobs and oversaw ministries at church. We spent time with friends and family. I still sensed life was lacking, but I couldn't deny life was good.

Lindsey called me on an unusually warm October afternoon. I had just come home from work, turned on the air-conditioning, and found Oprah on the television when the phone rang.

"Hi, Lindsey. It's been a while since we've heard from you. How is everything?" I was shaking a little, as I did every time she called, knowing she had the potential to make me a mom.

"Remember the baby we talked about a couple of months ago, the little girl with Down syndrome? We have a better grasp on her health issues now and wanted to see if you and your husband were interested in learning more."

I muted Oprah, started pacing around my house, and felt a giant smile spread across my face. "Yes. Definitely yes."

"Can you come into the office sometime in the next few days? A nurse will be here to share with you everything we know about the baby's health conditions."

"Oh, whoa. Okay. Sure." Somehow, since answering the phone, I had forgotten how to form a complete sentence.

"How about you talk to Josh and get back to me as soon as you can." Lindsey had no problem taking the reins on this phone conversation. I'm sure I was not the first speechless adoptive mother Lindsey had worked with.

I immediately called Josh, and we decided the least we could do was meet with the necessary people in the agency and hear more about this baby girl.

Before the appointment, Josh and I sat in our car in the underground parking lot of our adoption agency's office building. Neither of us wanted to make the first move, so we sat.

I broke the silence with my pragmatic pep talk. "It's just an informational meeting. Just informational."

"You're right. This meeting is not a yes or a no." My optimistic husband was leaning hard into my pragmatic thinking.

"Okay then, let's go."

As we made our way up to the third floor, the nerves began to set in. Lindsey met us in the lobby, and we followed her to a small room. Already seated in metal folding chairs were the head of the adoption agency, a social worker for the birth family, a separate social worker for the baby, and the agency's nurse. We sat in the chairs set up for us.

"Josh and Heather, thank you so much for coming," said Deborah, a striking woman with mocha brown skin and gentle eyes. Deborah ran the agency with the perfect mixture of class and grit. "As you know, this baby had heart surgery a couple of months ago and she did very well. We now have a better grasp on her medical needs." Josh and I nodded, hanging onto her every word. Deborah continued talking. "In this meeting we'd like to present you with all the information we have about her and answer any questions you may have. Does that all sound good?"

We nodded our heads and watched her open a medical file two inches thick—for a three-month-old baby. We listened as each person present told us all they could about what they knew so far. I know for a fact that my chair was placed firmly on solid ground, but as each person spoke, I felt as though I was on an amusement park roller coaster. Each piece of information about this baby brought us either great joy or a lose-your-breath kind of fear. And when we thought we understood everything, again another bit of information they shared would jerk us to the left and then throw us to the right. There was so much to know about this tiny child.

But it was what we *didn't* know that truly terrified us. Not all of our questions had definitive answers.

We left with a stack of papers containing the important bits and told them we would do our best to make a decision in the next couple of days.

From there we drove to a burger place called Fuddruckers, because in a moment like this, I needed the comfort that only dishes full of gooey cheese sauce could offer.

With burgers, fries, and cheese sauce in hand, Josh and I sat down and looked at one another.

"I just have to start by saying, *why*?" I picked up my fist and shook it in the air. "Why is this getting more and more complicated with each new step? Why can't we have an easy yes? Ugh! I'm so frustrated."

"And this!" Josh put down his burger and picked up the heavy medical file. "I just want to say yes to adopting this baby girl, but this!" He shook the file the way I'd shaken my fist.

"I know. Who raises their hand and says, 'I want a medically fragile child. I want a child who needs heart surgery. I want a child on oxygen. A child who may not get better'?"

Josh joined in my rant. "Or how about, 'I want a child with Down syndrome'? Who signs up for a child with Down syndrome?"

We both sat in silence. I dipped a fry in the cheese sauce and took a bite. "All of that's true, but so is what we decided in Greece. At the center of all this is a baby. A sweet, tiny baby girl who needs a mom and dad. A baby." My posture softened.

"I know. And Heather, I really believe we can do this." My optimistic husband was back. "Let's pray about it and talk to people we trust. We'll figure it out." He reached across the table and gave my hand a reassuring squeeze. "But first, this burger."

It was difficult to believe that God's best for me in this season of my life was something so downright foolish in the eyes of the world. That his best may be the very thing I wanted with all my heart to avoid. That his best is often what the world tries to convince us is our worst.

The days following our meeting with the adoption agency were heavy and gray with rain. The weight of the decision at hand was like an elephant asleep on my chest, making it difficult to breathe deeply or think about anything else. Every day, our social worker and I exchanged questions and answers through e-mail. At one point during our back and forth, she assured me that if we decided not to adopt this baby, they would find her a good home. "It isn't your job to rescue her," she said. She reminded us that if we did not adopt this baby, we would soon get a different child. One with forty-six chromosomes and a whole heart. And while I think she said these words to offer us some kind of relief, they had the opposite effect on me.

For me, saying yes to a sick, suffering baby who would never have a family if not for us would be much easier than saying yes while knowing we weren't the only option for this child's happiness and well-being. I was constantly tempted by the thought of a healthy and whole child waiting for us just around the corner—maybe next month, or even the following week. At times, it seemed as though a yes to this baby was also a no to what we thought we wanted. A no to a deep, deep desire for a healthy son or daughter. But at this point in our journey, God was trying to open our eyes to the fact that a yes to him is the only yes we should ever be saying.

After a few days of exchanges with Lindsey, and us spending every hour of free time researching the medical conditions in this baby girl's file, she presented us with a helpful idea. She suggested we meet with the baby's cardiologist to get a better feel for what this little girl would be facing health-wise in the short and long term. The baby had an appointment with her cardiologist scheduled for October 8, and we could meet with him after he had seen her. Josh and I agreed.

In the weeks leading up to this meeting, God had seemed silent. I had never known a time in my life when I needed his crystal-clear direction and voice more, but all I heard from him was a big fat silence.

The day before this meeting, I would have welcomed a few innocent butterflies in my stomach. Instead, I felt as though an army of African fire ants were digging tunnels throughout my body. I was so nervous. The most frustrating thing was I wasn't sure what I was nervous about. I just knew I wanted—no, needed—some clarity on how to move forward with the adoption of this little girl.

That evening, Josh and I packed a picnic dinner and headed to our favorite park.

It was as warm as any night in the summer would be, but the earlier descent of the sun reminded us we were in the middle of fall. We pulled into the park and made our way across the grass to a huge jacaranda tree in the middle of the lawn. I pulled a light striped sheet out of our picnic basket and laid it out while Josh opened up two camping chairs. We sat down, unfolded the paper wrapped around our sandwiches, and pulled out a container of fruit.

"Well, what do you think?" Josh asked.

"I think this not-knowing-what-to-do thing sucks. I think I need a little clarity." I held up the container of fruit, offering some to him. "What do *you* think?"

"I agree. Hopefully tomorrow, after meeting with the doctors, we will have just that." Josh popped a grape into his mouth.

"What if that's not the case? What if we leave the doctor's office knowing nothing new? I don't know how much longer I can sit on this middle ground. I'm frustrated that God's not making things clear."

"How about this?" Josh lifted his eyes to the heavens and said, "God, if you want us to adopt this child, then tomorrow there will be some kind of good news from the cardiologist. If the answer to adopting this child is no, then tomorrow there will be only bad news."

I gave him a sly grin when he lowered his eyes. "You think you can make God talk?"

"If you want to see it that way. We can't hear his voice in this situation, so why not set it up so we can?" Josh took a confident bite out of his sandwich.

"Okay. Then amen and amen." I lovingly rolled my eyes, hopeful that God had taken our prayer into consideration.

As I look back on that conversation we had with God, I can see just how little Josh and I knew him then. Just how little I understood what is important in life. Just how easily I could have missed out on the best of the best of the best because I believed that God's best for my life could only be found down a smooth road.

I prepared for the meeting with the cardiologist, believing that God wanted the same things for me that I wanted for myself. Our prayer made sense to me because I didn't see how God could want us to step into a no-good-news situation. I had placed him—the one true, omniscient, omnipresent, powerful God—on the same level as myself. I was forgetting that not only does God want my life to be greater than I can even begin to plan for, but he is the coach and writer and director and everything. He is everything!

My phone rang as we pulled into the hospital parking lot. It was Lindsey.

"Heather, there's been a slight change in plans. Everyone is running way behind, so the baby is still here. She hasn't even had her echocardiogram yet."

This was a *big* change in plans. We were scheduled to see the cardiologist after he got the results of the baby's echocardiogram—an ultrasound that would examine the condition of her heart.

"If you want to come up, you can meet the baby and her foster mom and hear what the doctor has to say, or you can come back when they're done. It's totally up to you."

Meeting the baby was risky. Our social worker had set the

appointment for after the baby's testing was finished, because in her professional experience she knew that often all bets were off once the baby, who had existed for the adoptive parents only on paper, was seen as a living, breathing, adorable human. Even knowing that, meeting the baby was still a no-brainer for me. Josh agreed.

"Yes! We'll come up."

We trusted our ability to separate our logic from our emotions. As we stepped into the hospital, what was going to be a simple meeting with a cardiologist turned into the day we met our daughter.

When the automatic doors at the children's hospital opened for us and we stepped into the foyer, we had no idea how familiar this place would soon become. Directly in front of us was an information desk with a kind-eyed woman sitting behind it. Large waiting areas flanked either side of the entrance. Lining the walls were brightly colored seats and benches full of people waiting to hear about their loved ones in surgery. The elevators faced a gift shop full of toys, books, and a huge bundle of get-well balloons at the entrance. Near the elevator we saw Lindsey wave at us.

"The baby is here with her foster mom," she told us as we rode the elevator to the second floor. "They've been waiting for over an hour and should be called back soon. Sorry this is taking so long."

"It's no problem," I said. "I'm excited to meet her." But as we turned the corner, I felt that all-too-familiar feeling of those African fire ants marching, marching, marching. The waiting area was packed with babies in strollers or on their parents' laps. Children swarmed a plastic playhouse in the corner, while a few kids in wheelchairs watched cartoons on the TV. I scanned the room, anxious to see the baby who brought us there in the first place. We followed Lindsey to a lovely blond woman holding a baby who had an unnatural amount of crazy brown hair.

"Josh, Heather, this is Sandy, and this"—she leaned down and held the hand of the crazy-haired baby—"is Arpi." The Armenian name given to her by her birth parents.

"Nice to meet you, Sandy." I smiled at the foster mom and then shifted my attention to the baby in her arms. "Hi, sweet girl."

"Do you want to hold her?" And just like that, this baby I'd been so terrified of was in my arms, and she wasn't scary at all.

I would love to tell you that I knew right then she was my daughter. I would love for our story to be one of love at first sight, but I think those stories mostly happen in the movies. Truth was, I was in protection mode. My heart had been through so much thus far, and so I didn't want it to fall for the scrumptious baby peering up at me with almond eyes and a button nose. I was thrilled to meet her, and she felt so good in my arms—arms that had been empty for far too long. But I did not feel like her mother at that moment. I wouldn't let my emotions get the best of me, for logic seemed the most, well, logical response, given the situation.

Sandy interrupted my thoughts. "She's such a sweet girl."

"She's adorable," Josh said. He stood by my side, holding her perfect and tiny hand.

Within minutes of meeting this beautiful baby girl, a nurse came and called her back for her echocardiogram. Sandy invited me to go in with her for the procedure. Only two adults were allowed at the bedside, so my husband graciously stayed in the crowded waiting area.

The procedure room was dimly lit and included a hospital bed, a huge piece of equipment with buttons and lights and a screen, and an ultrasound wand that would let us see through her skin and bones to her sick little beating heart. Sandy laid Arpi on the bed. She undressed the baby down to her diaper, and then the technician did a tricky blanket maneuver that swaddled Arpi's arms but left her bare chest exposed. At that point, the technician began applying stickers with tiny knobs to Arpi's chest and abdomen and squeezed a big gloppy squirt of the gel used to help the ultrasound wand glide over her tiny chest.

This whole time, I stood by the bedside with the baby's tiny fingers wrapped around mine. I had a million questions but tried to ask only a few. The procedure was painless, they explained. I watched the technician's every move and tried to breathe in this new world of tubes and hospital beds and complicated machines. I felt the urge to act as this baby's mom but knew Sandy had been playing that role for almost three months. I wanted to respect her and not step on any toes.

Still, I watched the wand move around on Arpi's tiny chest and wondered if she could be mine. Josh and I knew we would name our first child Macyn. As the baby dozed off to the hum of medical machines, I gazed at her precious round face and rosebud lips and wondered, *Could she be a Macyn? Is she my Macyn?* And while I had vowed to let logic control this day, I found myself leaning over the hospital bed and gently whispering in her ear, just to see what it would feel like.

"Hello, Macyn."

When the echocardiogram was complete and the technician had gotten all the necessary pictures of her heart, all of us walked from the children's hospital wing to the heart institute in the main hospital, where we would meet with the cardiologist, Dr. Kuhn.

My husband and I held one another's sweaty hands tightly now. We remembered the prayer we had prayed the night before, and we were trusting and believing the news the cardiologist was about to share with us would confirm whether we should say yes or no to adopting this baby girl.

Sandy and Arpi saw Dr. Kuhn first, and then it was our turn.

"We have to go now," Sandy said with kind eyes and a sweet smile before we went in. "I have to pick my daughter up from school."

Josh and I each gave her a big hug. Then we looked down at the baby peering up at us from her stroller. I gently brushed her soft cheeks with the back of my hand.

"Bye, sweet girl. It was so nice to meet you and hold you." I leaned down and kissed her forehead, and then we watched them walk away.

Josh and I timidly entered Dr. Kuhn's office. He was younger than I expected and super cool. He could have been in his late forties or early fifties, but his face looked youthful, and he had a small diamond earring in one of his ears.

I am a friendly person. I like small talk, and when I meet others, I would rather give them a hug than shake their hand. As we entered this doctor's office, I was hoping he felt the same. I wanted a warm and fuzzy meeting about how wonderful this baby was and how wonderful we were for thinking about adopting her. I wanted him to put his arm around our shoulders and tell us that, although she was very sick right now, everything would be okay.

But it wasn't, and he didn't.

"Hi, come on in. Have a seat." He motioned toward the only two chairs in the room. Then he got down to business. He pulled out a notepad with a drawing of an anatomically correct heart on it.

"This is what a heart is supposed to look like." Then he opened a pen and began to draw on the paper. "This is what Arpi's heart looks like." The differences were apparent. "There are a few things going on here. She has a hole that will need to be fixed called an atrial septal defect." He circled part of the picture of the heart. Josh and I listened and watched.

Dr. Kuhn continued. "This hole is causing high pressure in her lungs, because the oxygenated and nonoxygenated blood is not going where it should. This can cause pulmonary hypertension, which Arpi has."

Pulmonary hypertension was the nasty and terrifying condition we read in her medical file and had been trying to learn more about. It occurs when the blood flow that leaves the right side of the heart faces an increased pressure. Sometimes there is no obvious cause; other times it can be caused by certain types of congenital heart defects. While it can be treated with oxygen and a variety of medications, there is no cure for pulmonary hypertension.

"Oftentimes, pulmonary hypertension is a secondary condition caused by the hole in one's heart," the doctor explained. "This is not the case for Arpi. The levels of pressure in her lungs are so severe I'm not sure if patching the hole will help at all."

The fire ants began their march.

For the millionth time since we started this adoption journey, I felt sick. This was bad news. I took a deep breath and found the words to ask him a question, "So if you think the surgery will not help much with the pulmonary hypertension, what can be done to fix that? What kind of life are we talking about for this baby girl?"

With a solemn look, he spoke the words I had been dreading. "Honestly, there is nothing that can be done for pulmonary hypertension. If the heart surgery doesn't fix the problem—and with levels as high as hers, it most likely will not—then you are looking at quality-of-life care. She may live to be five, maybe as old as eight. It's really hard to say."

I have little memory of what happened after that. As Josh and I left his office and the automatic hospital doors ushered us outside, all I could think was, *She may live to be five, maybe as old as eight . . . maybe as old as eight.*

As soon as we got in the car, Josh spoke up. "I know we told God bad news would mean we wouldn't adopt her, but I can't say no. No just cannot be the answer."

I nodded my head in agreement but still lacked the words to join the conversation.

We left the hospital and silently drove to Costco to pick up a few items. By the time we pulled into the parking lot, we were both in tears. Tears of fear, pain, and frustration. Tears of longing, and even a few tears of joy at having met Arpi that day. We sat there in the car weeping and trying to make sense of it all. So much about the situation was, once again, out of this control freak's control. I remembered I could say no.

I can say no!

Then a whisper. A vision of sorts. I looked at my husband in the driver's seat of our car. Josh wore his sunglasses, but I knew behind them his eyes were swollen with tears. I grabbed his hand.

"What if God is giving us a gift?" I said. "I feel as though God has handed us a package wrapped up in sparkly paper topped with ribbons and bows. I see us opening that gift and looking at it with disgust and then handing it back to God, telling him it's not what we asked for and we don't want it. Josh, I see us handing a gift that God has given us back to him. Back to God. Who does that? I think this baby is our gift, and I think we would be fools to hand her back."

And with those words, I felt a flood of relief. Saying no to adopting this baby always made the most sense. She was sick, really sick. She might not live long. She required high levels of medical attention and care. Oh yeah, and she had Down syndrome. No was a perfectly acceptable answer.

We had spent weeks creating formulas to help us make this difficult decision. We had prayed about it and sought wisdom from loved ones we trusted. But rather than offer our whole hearts to God, we were giving him ultimatums. Rather than simply saying, "Yes, God!

I want what you want," we were telling him how to fix the situation so it would look a certain way before we could join him in it.

There in that parking lot, God was showing me she was a gift. Not just any gift, but one handed to us by God himself, wrapped in sparkly paper, for goodness' sake. He was showing us this baby girl was not a no. He was beginning to teach us that difficult decisions could be answered with, "We want what God wants. We say yes to him."

We called our social worker.

"Lindsey, it's Heather. We're going to adopt Arpi."

Coming To Grips

When we first began our journey toward parenthood, I dreamed of the moment when I would reveal my positive pregnancy test to my whole family and close circle of friends. I would gather everyone around and begin my big reveal with, "Guess what, everyone?" I imagined we would all jump up and down with tears of joy as loved ones wrapped their arms around my neck and rubbed my soon-to-be bulging belly. We would begin to talk about baby names and whether we'd prefer a boy or a girl. Before a bump would even show, we would gather new furniture, paint walls, assemble cribs, and hang tiny clothes on tiny hangers. We would watch my belly grow as we attended baby showers thrown for us by friends and family. I had it all planned out.

By the time Josh and I called our social worker and said yes to adopting this crazy-haired baby girl, I had let go of my dream of holding up a positive pregnancy test and sharing the news with the world. It pained me to let go of the moment I could see so clearly in my head, a moment I had anticipated over and over. A moment that would never come to be.

As we began our adoption journey, I was able to replace my desire to announce a pregnancy with a new hope and vision. Instead of a positive pregnancy stick, I would have a phone call from our social worker telling us about the birth mother who had just chosen us to parent her child. I imagined ending that call and excitedly calling everyone I knew to share the great news. I would start with my parents, of course: "Guess what, Mom and Dad? You're going to be grandparents!" Everything else would proceed as planned: the jumping up and down, the tears of joy, the furniture, the clothes . . .

When Josh and I sat in the Costco parking lot, our eyes full of tears, once again my ideas of how I would announce my motherhood were taken from me. True, I would make the phone calls and let everyone know we were going to be parents, but the news did not end there.

Josh and I abandoned our shopping plans and drove across the street to a coffee shop. Josh stayed in the car and called his parents from his phone. I got out, sat on a bench outside the shop, and dialed my dad's office.

"Hello, this is Kim."

"Hi, Dad. It's me."

"Elizabeth!" My dad often endearingly calls me by my middle name. "How was the doctor's visit?"

My parents had been our biggest supporters and the two people Josh and I went to the most often for wisdom and prayer. They were aware of everything that had led up to our visit with the cardiologist.

The news I had expected to shout from the rooftops came out as a faint, weepy whisper. "Well, you guys are going to be grandparents."

Dad's phone was on speaker, and my mom chimed in. "What happened?" She knew me well enough to hear the sorrow and confusion in my voice. The tears I cried then were not tears of joy.

"It was all bad news. There was no good news. She's really sick." I took a deep breath to help me regain my composure. I did not want this moment to be shadowed by any kind of sorrow. "But we really believe she is a gift from God, so we are saying yes to her."

"Well, Heather"—my mom sounded confused—"you don't have to, you know."

"Mom!" I got up from the bench and began to pace. "I really just need your trust and support here."

"You have it, Heather. You have my support, but can you tell us what the doctor said?"

"It was a lot. I'd rather talk in person. Can we come to the office?"

I had a feeling defending our decision to adopt this little girl was going to be exhausting. "How long will you guys be there?"

"We're here as long as you need," my dad said. "Come anytime."

It was only a five-minute drive to my dad's office, but somehow time played tricks on me, and the drive seemed to take hours. When we walked into the building, I did a little shoulder shake and put on a big smile in hopes of injecting a positive tone into our situation. I needed a smile. I deserved a smile, for goodness' sake. Josh held my hand, but holding tight to my other hand was somberness, the kind of thing that cannot be hidden from one's parents. We turned the corner and stood in the doorway of my dad's office.

After years of trying in vain to become a mother, I found myself at the water's edge, but the water before me was not the calm stream I believed I deserved. It was a raging ocean. Rather than jumping in with abandon, I thought I had to dodge the waves.

I would soon learn the need I felt to defend our decision and convince people of our future daughter's worth came from within myself. In the days that followed our big scary yes, I was the one who needed the most convincing that we'd made the right choice.

I made eye contact with my mom, and the tears began to flow again.

"Oh, Heather!" She ran to my side with a mother's embrace. Arm in arm we walked to the old orange leather couch and sat down. I grabbed a throw pillow and hugged it to my chest, searching for comfort in any form. Josh and I took deep breaths and began to retell everything we had just learned about this baby girl with Down syndrome.

"I just don't want you to feel like you need to rescue this baby," my mom said. "Heather, I know your heart. You've always wanted to rescue the underdog, but this is different. This is a really big deal."

"I know it's a big deal." I was feeling irritated by her pushback. "I need you to trust who you raised me to be. I need you to trust that

Josh and I understand the magnitude of this decision." I felt my throat begin to close up and my eyes well with tears.

My dad saw how tense the situation was becoming and spoke up. "The word I keep hearing is *grips*," he said. "At first I thought we needed to come to terms with the situation. But while praying over you, God told me this isn't about coming to terms with what's happening, but rather coming to grips with it."

He explained: "When you come to terms with something, two parties present their case and make compromises until an agreement is reached that everyone accepts. The situation with this baby is not one of coming to terms. This isn't the kind of situation we bring before God with an expectation that he will compromise. Adopting this baby does not hinge on our terms. The Lord is showing me we need to look at what God is calling you to, calling all of us to, and grip it tightly with both hands."

"You're right, Kim," my mom said as she squeezed my hand.

"Thank you, Dad," I whispered through tears, but this time tears full of hope and peace.

As we headed home that evening, I began to think about the difference between coming to terms and coming to grips. I thought about all the times I had failed to grip the thing God placed in front of me or the thing he allowed to pass through my door. How many times had I made demands about what God was calling me to do? How many more times would I try to negotiate God's best rather than grip what was right in front of me, no matter how terrifying?

Friends, we are talking about God. *God*, who loves us more than we can ever understand. *God*, who wants more goodness and wholeness for our lives than we could ever want for ourselves. What a fool I am when I look at what God is calling me to and say, straight to his face, "Okay, God, I'll think about it, but only if . . ."

We said yes to adopting our daughter! We said yes! As an act of tightly gripping her and the situation at hand, we named her Macyn Hope, a name we had been holding on to for our firstborn. She was no longer "the baby girl with Down syndrome" or "Arpi." She was Macyn Hope . . . *our* Macyn Hope.

We said yes on October 8, 2008, and Macyn came home to be ours on October 28. Those twenty days between were an emotional whirlwind. While we gripped our yes as tightly as we could, numerous were the moments in which we wanted to let go. I was still feeling as though God had remained mostly silent. True, I had the vision of him handing us a gift, but I began to wonder if I had made it all up.

On October 10, I headed to Oceanside to celebrate my mom's birthday. My parents had rented a condo on the beach and invited us to stay with them for the weekend. Josh had some work to do, so I went ahead of him. He would meet up with us the next day.

The following morning, I sat on the deck of the second-story condo with a steamy mug of coffee in my hands and a blanket wrapped around my shoulders. The sun had come up, but the sky was thick with a blanket of coastal fog. Hours would pass before the sun broke through. I sat there thinking about the decision we had made, still feeling pricks of doubt. Yet as I listened to the waves crash on the shore, I tightly gripped God's bigness, knowing he is greater and stronger than any kind of sickness Macyn might face. I trusted he was holding my daughter tightly even at that moment.

"Hey, Elizabeth." My dad stepped out onto the patio. "Josh is on the phone."

I took my phone from my dad. "How's it going?"

He got right to the point. "Have you read today's Oswald?" A favorite daily devotional of ours is *My Utmost for His Highest* by Oswald Chambers, which we often refer to simply as Oswald.

"Not yet, why?"

"Oh, Heather, it's a word straight from God to us. Just go read it and call me back."

"Okay, I'll call you in a bit."

I went into the condo to get my devotional. I opened to October 11, and the title jumped off the page: "After God's Silence, What?" I went on to read, "Has God trusted you with a silence—a silence that is big with meaning? God's silences are His answers . . . If God has given you a silence, praise Him, He is bringing you into the great run of His purposes.'"*

I read and reread the passage, each word speaking directly to my heart. And just like that, his silence was broken. Could it be God was silent because he had already equipped me to make the right decision?

I returned home from my weekend at the beach with the clarity and confidence I needed to move forward in our adoption of Macyn. The clouds that had been hanging over our heads since we learned about this baby began to part, and the doubts in my heart made way for a mother's bright joy.

When we announced to friends and loved ones that the baby we were adopting had Down syndrome, you could see the confusion and discomfort on their faces, but we didn't let it get to us. We simply smiled and said something along the lines of, "Not many people get a child with Down syndrome. Aren't we lucky?"

---

* Oswald Chambers, *My Utmost for His Highest Classic Edition* (Grand Rapids: Discovery House, 2011), October 11.

Because Macyn had spent almost three months in a foster home, we transitioned her slowly to placement in our home. The purpose of a slow transition was to make sure Macyn didn't feel she'd been thrown into the arms of strangers. We spent days going back and forth between our home and our daughter's foster home for "visits." During these visits, we got to know our new baby girl. More importantly, she got to know us. We learned how to turn on the oxygen tank and why it was important to let all the oxygen out before turning it off. We filled up tiny syringes with nasty-tasting medication, and her foster mom showed us how to best administer it. But mostly we held her in our arms and stared at her perfect little face.

During these days of preparing for Macyn to come home and be ours forever, our social worker let us know that Macyn's birth parents would need to sign relinquishment papers. It is illegal in the United States for parents to abandon their children, so those creating an adoption plan cannot relinquish their rights until there is a family in place to adopt the child.

The day before Macyn's birth parents were scheduled to sign their relinquishment, our social worker called to tell us about what would take place. There was nothing unusual about this procedure, Lindsey said. She did not expect any complications, because the birth parents had chosen to place Macyn in foster care until a family was found. The people who had given her life hadn't seen her or inquired about her for almost three months. She would call us when the paperwork was complete.

The next day, I woke up feeling anxious. As I got ready for work and drove to the school, I could think of nothing else but getting that phone call.

It wasn't even lunchtime when my phone rang, and the caller ID flashed Lindsey's name. I held my breath and picked up the phone.

"We've had a bit of a setback," she said. "Don't worry, it's not a big deal, but the parents don't want to sign relinquishment without meeting you and Josh."

I was in shock. Meeting the birth parents was never on my agenda. "Are they going to change their minds?"

"I really don't think so. They just don't understand why you would want to adopt their daughter, and they have some questions for you."

"What kind of questions? Lindsey, this makes me nervous."

"Don't worry. It's completely normal for adoptive parents and birth parents to meet. This happens all the time. We just hadn't expected it in your case."

We set a time to meet that afternoon, and then I hung up and quickly called Josh.

"I don't understand," he said. "Are they changing their minds?"

"Lindsey doesn't think so. But what if they are?"

I officially started to freak out. We had been a part of this adoption world long enough to hear parents' heartbreaking stories of being chosen for a child, only to have the birth parents change their minds. It's a reality of adoption. The child you have longed for, the one you fall in love with and think about constantly, is not legally and officially and finally yours until the final adoption papers are signed—and that can take months, sometimes even years. Once the birth parents sign relinquishment papers or have their rights terminated, it's rare for an adoptive family to lose the child. However, the first few weeks and months, especially before relinquishment papers are signed, are fragile. Any number of complications might snatch this baby girl out of our arms before she was even able to fill them, and birth parents changing their minds was at the top of that list.

When the school bell rang for lunch, I had about an hour until my next group of students would be in their desks. I couldn't handle feeling out of control any longer, so I did the only thing I could think of: I jumped into my car and drove to a local shopping center.

A social worker once informed Josh and me that it was customary for an adoptive parent to get a small gift for the birth parent. This custom sprang from the idea that when an adoptive parent walks away with a baby in her arms, the birth mother's arms are empty. While a small gift or token can never replace a baby, it's nice for a birth mother to walk away with something. We would not be taking Macyn home today. She was still living with the foster family, and this meeting with the birth parents was only a necessary step toward bringing her home—at least I hoped. But I drove to the shopping center anyway because I like to buy gifts. I am good at giving gifts, and I have control over gift giving. Just then, I needed some control.

I chose a store full of knickknacks and sentimental tokens. Twenty minutes later, I found myself circling the store for the hundredth time. I must have picked up and put back fifty items. Nothing felt right. What do you give to the people who are giving you their baby? I didn't know the answer, but after thirty minutes of shopping, I came to the conclusion that such a gift does not exist. I kept picking up sweet and heartfelt items and imagined myself saying, "Thank you for giving me your baby; here's a heart-shaped pillow in return." Or, "Thank you for the baby; here's a piece of jewelry." It just felt so strange.

I was feeling defeated and sick to my stomach about the meeting that would take place in a few hours, but I refused to leave that store empty-handed. With my heart on the ground and my stomach in my throat, I spotted, out of the corner of my eye, a colorful string of fabric birds. Birds! We had decided on a bird theme for Macyn's room, and this decoration would fit perfectly. I thought about giving a string of these same birds to Macyn's birth parents and telling them that Macyn had a matching set. She would wake up every morning with them hanging above her bed as though they'd flown in to greet her for the day. I would invite them to hang the string of birds in their home as well, a symbolic way for us to remain connected.

It was the best I could do, so I grabbed two sets and proceeded to the register.

A few hours later, Josh and I pulled into the parking garage at our adoption agency's office building. We were about twenty minutes early. We punched in the code for the gate and drove to the basement parking area. I found myself scanning the dimly lit lot, nervous about running into the birth parents before we were scheduled to meet in our social worker's office. I dreaded the thought of riding in an elevator with them. I'm not good at silence, and I could just picture myself saying something like, "So, you're giving us your baby, huh?" Or, "Sure do hope you give us your baby; here's a string of fabric birds." But I didn't see anyone else getting out of their car, so we hurried inside.

Lindsey met us as we stepped out of the elevator.

"What's this meeting really about?" Josh asked as we followed her to her office.

"It's common for birth parents to want to meet the adoptive parents. It just normally happens before the baby is born."

"Are they going to change their minds?" I blurted out again.

"I really don't think so. They haven't seen the baby since she was born and haven't shown a desire to parent her. But as you know, there are no guarantees at this stage."

Really? No guarantees? Our social worker had always been to the point and never sugarcoated things, but these were not the reassuring words I was hoping to hear.

We entered Lindsey's tiny office. An interpreter was already present. Macyn's birth parents are Armenian, and English is not their first language. Given the gravity of the situation at hand, I was thankful to have an interpreter help us communicate our best intentions. We smiled at her and exchanged pleasantries.

Josh and I sat side by side on a small, black leather couch. In front of us was a coffee table with pens and a box of tissues on it. Circling the coffee table were chairs for everyone to sit in. We weren't holding hands because our hands were too sweaty for that. I watched as the clock on the wall above the door read 5:00, then 5:15, 5:20. Every minute ticked painfully by. Finally, we heard some commotion out in the foyer. I heard three voices, thick accents, apologies, and explanations involving traffic. Then the birth parents' social worker entered the room, followed by Macyn's birth parents.

I will forever remember my first meeting with Vickie and Kaapo. I can't say I felt at ease when they came in, but there was something about their presence that gave me a sense of calm. As we shook hands and said our hellos, I suddenly began to think about how they must be feeling. How the past few months must have been for them. I could see brokenness in their eyes, and it broke me.

I had found myself at times critical of some birth parents who surrender their children, including Macyn's. How could someone choose an adoption plan over parenting their own flesh and blood? But as we sat down with this couple, compassion overwhelmed me. I believed they were doing the best they could with what they knew and what they had. To me these two people were no longer just "Macyn's birth parents." Now they were Kaapo and Vickie.

As they took their seats in the chairs across from us, I noticed both Kaapo and Vickie were an inch or two shorter than I am. Their olive-toned skin, dark eyes, and dark hair instantly took me back to the Eastern European country that had stolen my heart just months ago. Vickie was about ten years older than me, and Kaapo ten years older than her. Kaapo wore glasses that sat crooked on his face, the arm for his left ear missing. They both spoke with thick accents but made an effort to speak English as much as they could. As our time went on, I learned that Vickie had an infectious laugh.

Lindsey had told us in advance to ask as many questions as we could think of. She said many times adoptive and birth parents meet only once, so it's important to try to ask questions the child might want to know answers to as she gets older. So I sat through the meeting with a notebook in my lap, writing down bits of information. Some of it seemed extremely important. Macyn has three half siblings living in Armenia, and Kaapo and Vickie have a daughter who is only eighteen months older than Macyn. Other bits of information didn't hold the same weight but felt important anyway. Vickie's favorite food is dolma (one of my favorite foods as well). She loves to dance, and she danced a lot while she was pregnant with Macyn.

Kaapo spoke at length about his love for his home country. He told us how beautiful the land was and how proud he was to be an Armenian man. We assured him Macyn's heritage was important to us, and that we'd like to learn more about it and incorporate it into her life as much as possible.

After an hour or so of conversation, a hush came over the room.

"Tell us about the name Arpi," Josh asked, knowing we would be changing her name.

Kaapo answered through the interpreter. "Arpi is a common Armenian name meaning 'sun.'"

"We think it's a beautiful name, but we've always wanted to name our first child Macyn. We want to give her that name." I began to fidget with a string on my pants. "If it's okay with you."

They looked to the translator as she told them what I said and then looked at me with gracious smiles.

"Macyn is a beautiful name," Vickie said in her best English.

Again, silence. We were letting the birth parents lead the conversation, so we waited. Finally, Kaapo spoke up.

"We want her to know us. We want to see her. I can be like her uncle."

With this request, I realized their idea of adoption was not the 2008 American idea of what an adoption looks like. They had been in the country less than ten years and were living in a part of Los Angeles that was basically Little Armenia. They were still steeped in the culture and ways of their home country. I was beginning to realize that Kaapo and Vickie needed to meet with us because they were afraid we would take their child and never tell her about where she had come from. They needed to be certain she would know about her Armenian roots, about her sister, and about the people who gave her life. I saw a fear in Kaapo that we would never let them see her again. Kaapo offered to be an "uncle" in case we wanted to keep the truth of who they were a secret.

"Kaapo," I quickly replied, "we will always tell Macyn who she is and where she came from. This adoption will not be a secret."

Josh added, "You will always be her birth father, and, Vickie, you will always be her birth mother. And we will tell her about you with love and pride. She will know who you are, because who you are is a huge piece of who she is."

The interpreter repeated all of this in Armenian. Kaapo's face softened, and his eyes welled with tears.

"Thank you." I could see our response to his concern was a huge relief.

As we began to wrap up our time together, Vickie asked me to write down their address and phone number. I glanced at Lindsey, knowing information like this is highly classified in most adoptions. She didn't seem to have any concerns. I uncomfortably wrote down their address and phone number. Then they asked for ours.

At this point, they didn't even know our last name, and as far as I was concerned, I was going to keep it that way. When I woke up that morning, I was planning on nothing more than exchanging pictures and letters with our daughter's birth parents through the adoption agency. Now we had agreed to let them be a part of our lives. I wasn't ready for them to know where we lived.

"I hope this doesn't offend you, but we'd like to get to know you better first." I looked at their faces as they listened to the interpreter.

Kaapo was quick to reply. "Oh yes, of course. That is fine."

Lindsey said, "If no one has any more questions, I think this meeting went really well."

"Nope, no more questions here." Josh and I were emotionally spent and wanted to head home.

We all stood to leave, shook hands, and said our good-byes, and then I gave them their gift. Josh and I headed to the car. Kaapo and Vickie stayed behind to sign the relinquishment papers.

Of course, at the time we had no idea where this customary meeting would eventually lead. But by then, we would be much better equipped to come to grips with just about anything God put in front of us.

5

Life in the
Shadow of Death

When Macyn came home at three months old, you can bet I had a stack of books with expert advice on babies, as well as on babies with Down syndrome. I perused the web to help fill in the gaps the books failed to address. In addition, I had my own ideas on what would be best for our baby. I pieced together the highest quality information I could find to form my own "manual," if you will.

Prior to becoming a mom, I had tons of experience with children of all ages. I began babysitting at a young age and was a nanny throughout college. I was a pro diaper changer and could calm even the fussiest of babies. I felt confident in my ability to be a top-notch mom even without the stack of books by my bed, but I appreciated the expert advice.

Enter Macyn. She did not come with a book.

Placement day was a dream. Josh and I arrived home with Macyn in the early evening, the warm sun still shining in the October sky. We pulled into our driveway, and I smiled at the banner hanging from our garage: "Welcome Home, Macyn," painted in bright colors. I scooped our daughter out of her car seat while Josh used both hands to carry in the large, heavy oxygen concentrator.

We opened the front door to our home and were surprised by the evidence of our dearest friends, who had been sneaking in and out while we were away. Our dining room table was stacked with gifts wrapped in every shade of pink and purple, and the banister leading upstairs had a dozen or more sparkly balloons tied to it.

"Whoa! Look, baby girl!" I turned Macyn to see all the love that had been poured out for her. Josh carried the concentrator to her room and headed back to the car to get the cooler full of medications that needed constant refrigeration and the portable oxygen tanks.

"Who are all the gifts from?" Josh called over his shoulder as he transferred the meds from the cooler to the fridge.

"Our sweet friends." I picked up the large note atop the pile of gifts. "They said, 'Because your sweet Macyn shouldn't be around a lot of people, we present to you a people-less baby shower!'"

A knock sounded at the door.

"Where's our new granddaughter?" my mom and dad said in unison as they let themselves in. They gently charged toward us.

"Wait!" I turned so they couldn't touch the baby in my arms. "You have to wash your hands." Macyn's sick heart lowered her immunity, putting her at greater risk for illness. If she was to get a cold, it could instantly go to her lungs and cause pneumonia and lead to death—her doctor's words, not mine. So hand washing became a religious activity in our home.

After another knock at the door, my younger sister, Hana, came in with a bouquet of colorful balloons. "Hey, Heathy, where is my little niece?"

"Wait!" My mom yelled at her before she could even take a step. "You have to wash your hands."

We spent the next couple of hours opening gifts and passing around our perfect little daughter until it was her bedtime.

Josh headed toward the kitchen. "I'll get her medications and bottle ready."

I took Macyn from her grandpa's arms. "Say good night to your grandpa."

My dad brushed her hair from her forehead and gave her a kiss. "Good night, Macyn Hope. I'm so happy you're here." Then he gave me a goofy grin, his eyes brimming with tears.

I walked my daughter over to say good night to my mom and sister, who were sitting on our sectional couch, but they both stood.

"We're coming up with you," Hana announced, and they followed us up the stairs, Macyn's little head peeking over my shoulder.

I walked into Macyn's room, her walls painted in bold colors and bordered with the silhouette of little birds on a wire. I laid her down on her back on the padded changing table. She was already beginning to fall asleep. I gently removed her green onesie.

"Hana, will you grab the flowered sleeper from the top drawer?" She opened the dresser drawer and handed me the sleeper. I got Macyn into her jammies and began hooking her up to her oxygen. The oxygen she required was pumped into her tiny lungs through a tiny cannula in her tiny nose. This cannula was attached to some plastic tubing, which attached to a concentrator, which was plugged into the wall and hummed loudly when it was on. It was literally a lifeline. I carefully handed Macyn to my mom, who sat on the vintage olive-green chair in the corner of the room. My mom sang sweet lullabies from my childhood, and Macyn nodded off.

Josh came up, followed by my dad, with Macyn's medication and bottle. "She's already asleep?"

"It was a super long day for her," I said as we all gathered around our new girl and just stared.

"May I?" Josh looked to my mom and held out his arms for his daughter.

"Of course." My mom gently handed Macyn to Josh, careful not to wake her or get tangled up in the tubing. Josh sat in the green chair, switching places with my mom.

Mom put her arm around my waist. "We're going to go and let you three have this moment."

My dad came and kissed me on the head. "I'm so happy for you,

Elizabeth." Then he gave Josh a pat on the shoulder. "Congratulations, Daddy."

"She's perfect, you guys." Hana gave me a big squeeze. "Simply perfect."

"Thank you for coming and for the food and the gifts and . . . everything. Thank you for everything." I began to cry as we shared hugs, and then my family left.

I sat on the floor near the chair where Josh was slowly squeezing the bitter medication from the syringe into the back of Macyn's mouth. Our sleeping angel puckered up her face and began to cry.

"It's okay, sweetie; just a little more and you can have your bottle." Josh squeezed the last drop and quickly replaced the syringe with a warm bottle. "There you go, sweet girl," he whispered, and the sound of his voice and the warmth of the milk calmed her down.

When she finished her bottle, Josh placed her over my shoulder, and I bounced and gently patted her back. It couldn't have been more than five steps from the chair to her crib, but as I walked, I became tangled up in the tubing attached to her face.

"Whoa. Careful." Josh steadied me as I fumbled.

"That's going to take some getting used to." I made it safely to the crib and held my sleeping baby out so I could see her face. Behind me, Josh leaned over my shoulder. "She's finally here! I can't believe it. Thank you, Jesus!" Josh brushed the hair from Macyn's forehead and gave her a kiss. "Good night, my daughter."

I laid her on her back. "I love you, Macyn Hope."

Josh took the empty bottle downstairs to the kitchen, and I fell to my knees beside my daughter's crib. "Thank you, Jesus, for this baby. Thank you that I get to be her mom. Please, please, please, dear Jesus, protect her from the cord in her crib. Give her a strong heart and healthy and whole lungs. In Jesus' name. Amen."

Our nightly routines with Macyn continued in the way they had begun. Each night, I did my best to keep her safe. I kept her crib free of loose blankets, pillows, or stuffed animals that could cause her to suffocate while she slept and was still too small to control all of her movements. Though her crib was devoid of "dangerous" organic cotton blankets and killer Winnie-the-Pooh plush toys, she had to go to bed every night with that dang plastic tube attached to her beautiful face. How was *that* not a hazard?

For the first few months, I felt pretty confident that her inability to move would protect her from being strangled by the threatening yet lifesaving tubing. But it wasn't long before she began to roll over and move around more. I found myself a little sick and slightly terrified whenever I placed my sleeping angel in her crib. I skimmed my books and the Internet for "how to keep kids alive when they have to sleep with plastic tubing in their beds." As expected, my searches always turned up empty.

I had to give up so much control on my journey to becoming Macyn's mom. I had been forced, in all the best ways, to trust God with so much of my life. But this sleeping-with-oxygen thing took the surrender cake.

Every parent I know does everything in their power to keep their kids safe and alive. It's basically a parent's number-one job. Josh and I had to get creative to make sure the tubing never snaked its way around Macyn's neck. We used special tape to ensure the cannula would not slip from her nose. The tape would sometimes leave little sores on the tip of her nose or the side of her face, but we had to count the cost of keeping our daughter alive. We cut little holes in the feet of her pajamas and would feed the tubing down her back and through the hole to keep it as far from her neck as possible.

Every night before going to bed, I would check on Macyn dozens of times. I would check to make sure the tubing was where it should be. I would adjust her cannula, which so often slipped from her tiny nostrils. I would brush her crazy brown hair from her forehead, I would lean in and kiss her sweet button nose, and I would kneel at the side of her crib, my forehead to the floor, and plead with God. "Lord, heal my baby. Give her a strong beating heart; give her lungs that can function on their own; and keep the tubing in her crib from wrapping around her neck. In Jesus' name. Amen!"

Sometimes an acquaintance, someone who knew our situation but didn't really *know*, would comment about how stressful it must be to have my daughter sleep with tubing in her crib. "I wouldn't get any sleep if I were you. I'd be too worried the tubing would wrap around her neck." Then they would scoop up their perfectly healthy baby, and I would want to punch them in the face.

I never did.

Though these moms and friends made such comments in love, their ignorance sometimes led me to question my ability to keep my own child safe. Did the fact that I *could* sleep mean I was a bad mom? Over time, I became thankful for these kinds of conversations because they would always take me back to Jesus. In everything the Lord had been teaching me so far, I knew that trusting him was at the tippy-top of the list. I did everything within my control to make sure my daughter was as safe as she could be while she slept, but the real protection had to come from God.

And friends, this is the case for all parents. We have to hold on tightly to the truth that God loves our kiddos more than we ever will. We have to remember he is in control of their lives. These were the facts that helped me fall asleep at night, tubing and all.

Macyn's medication was a special liquid compound that could only be produced at special pharmacies, and it needed to be refrigerated at all times. Its bitterness could be neither sweetened nor flavored. This medication had to be given to Macyn four times a day: at six in the morning, noon, six in the evening, and finally at midnight. It was a most annoying way to keep track of the hours on the clock. Like the oxygen tubing, this medication became a necessary thorn in our side.

As the days, weeks, and months went on, I found my relationship with the oxygen and medication complicated at best. On the one hand, I hated them. I hated that they required me to alter my way of living. I hated what they represented: a sickness so great that we were at their mercy. And on the other hand, I loved them. I loved the comforting hum of her oxygen concentrator. I loved that the medication she needed was available to us. At midnight when my alarm would go off, I'd go to the refrigerator with heavy eyes, measure her medication, wake up my sleeping baby, and help her swallow the bitter liquid. While tired and annoyed, I would whisper a prayer of thanks.

I find it interesting and a tad bit obnoxious that life's necessary bitter things can offer so much needed goodness. I don't know about you, but I find myself waking up most mornings hoping for an easy day. A day free of the kind of tubing that may cause me to trip, a day free of any bitterness trying to find its way to my mouth. At the time, God was teaching me that sometimes those are the very things needed to keep us going, to keep us breathing, to keep us alive.

One month and three days after Macyn came home—one month and three days of being a mom, one month and three days of oxygen and medication—I found myself in the car on my way to the hospital for Macyn's open-heart surgery.

We knew about this surgery when we adopted Macyn. It was, in fact, one piece of medical information we received about her condition that didn't fill me with anxiety. I knew people whose children had successfully been through open-heart surgery. I felt as though I had a grasp on what it was, and being able to grasp anything in this season of life was a comfort.

The night before the surgery, we had prepared what we could. We set the timer on our coffeemaker and packed a little bag with clean clothes, snacks, books, Macyn's favorite blankets, and toys. We received comforting e-mails and phone calls offering prayers of peace, of guidance for the doctors, of miracles and healing. We huddled together as a family of three to sing songs and say prayers and kiss cheeks and stroke hair.

On the morning of December 1, 2008, we woke up while the stars were still dancing brightly in the sky, and we rubbed the sleep from our eyes under the light of the moon. The only thing we had left to do was wake our sleeping baby, bundle her up, gently strap her into her car seat, and head to the hospital.

Macyn was scheduled for the first surgery of the day. When we arrived, everything was quiet and still. As we made our way to the elevator and up to the second-floor pre-op room, I felt my grip on my baby tighten just a little, just enough to feel her sick little heart beating up against mine. We rode the elevator in silence, maybe because it was so early in the morning, or maybe because we didn't want to miss the sound of her every breath.

The elevator doors opened, and we stepped off. The hallways were silent and dimly lit. This was where we had our unexpected first meeting with Macyn just a few months earlier. Our familiarity with this place offered us a strange, unexpected peace. While we waited for the nurse to come get us, we took turns snuggling our baby girl, humming familiar songs and silently praying our guts out.

"Mr. and Mrs. Avis?" the nurse inquired with a kind smile.

"Yes, that's us." My heart began to beat faster.

"Follow me right this way."

We went through a single door off the waiting area to the pre-op room. Hospital beds lined the walls, each one waiting for a sick child to occupy its stiff, white sheets. Between the beds was an intermingling of bright, colorful murals of butterflies and smiling animals, and flashing or beeping medical equipment. The nurse led us to one of the beds.

"Here, put this on Macyn." She handed us the smallest hospital gown I had ever seen.

As I laid Macyn down and took off her cozy pajamas, I softly kissed her whole and scar-free chest. I tried to capture a memory of her just as she was in this moment. In less than an hour, they would take her from me, poke her with needles, attach her to machines, and cut open her chest. I wanted to remember her before all that happened to her tiny body. I gently touched her skin and could feel the bone that would soon be split open, and my eyes welled with tears—tears of love for this perfect human, and tears of fear for the unknown.

"Here, let me help." Josh came alongside and slipped one of Macyn's arms through the hole in the gown. I pulled the other through.

"This just got real," I said. I leaned on Josh and wrapped Macyn's fingers around one of mine. "You realize this surgery, the very thing she needs to save her life, could take it?"

"She's not going to die, Heather." Josh leaned down and kissed her cheeks. Macyn looked up at us and gave a sweet grin. "See, even *she* knows she'll be fine."

I laughed and wiped the tears from my eyes just as Macyn's surgeon approached, wearing blue scrubs and a colorful cap on his head.

"How is everyone today?" Dr. Razzouk asked as he placed his stethoscope over her heart.

"As good as can be expected, I guess." Josh gave my shoulder a squeeze.

"Do you have any last-minute questions for me?"

I wanted to shout, *Yes, of course, one million questions*, but instead said, "I know you've already explained the surgery to us, but could you give us a brief description of what's going to take place next?"

"Of course." He was calm and confident. "We will be patching a hole found between the chambers of her heart. She'll be placed on a heart-and-lung machine and will receive blood transfusions. Once the hole is patched, we'll stitch her up and send her to the fifth floor for a few days to recover."

"Are you ready for this surgery?" I asked. "Are you feeling confident?"

Dr. Razzouk, this surgeon sent by God, looked me in the eyes and said, "I am ready. I will be doing the best I can, but I am God's instrument being used to help your daughter. It is all in his hands."

The words I needed to hear allowed me to exhale.

Our thank-you was interrupted by a nurse. "Dr. Razzouk, the room is ready for you."

He gave us a nod. "The surgery will take about five hours. I'll meet with you as soon as it's over." And he walked away, disappearing through the heavy double doors at the far end of the room. Only seconds after he was gone, an anesthesiologist approached Macyn's bedside and introduced himself with a smile. "I'll be your daughter's anesthesiologist for the duration of the surgery. I will not leave her side. Has she been sick in the past forty-eight hours?"

"Nope. Super healthy, except for the hole in her heart. And her pulmonary hypertension." I gave the doctor a wink.

"Okay then, Mom and Dad. It's time."

Josh and I looked at each other and then at our happy little girl.

My heart sank. I was holding my daughter in a pre-op room. This could be the last time I would hold my new baby girl. The last time I would kiss her soft cheeks and smell the sweetness of her skin. When you cut open the chest of a nine-pound, frail, three-month-old baby, things can go wrong, and I knew that. This real-life moment staring me in the face, this anesthesiologist waiting for me to hand him my daughter, made me want to run out the door and hide.

Then God's still small voice reminded me to look at how far he had brought us. He reminded me to let him be God and do his thing. He reminded me that no matter the outcome of this surgery, he was still God, he was still good, and I am forever Macyn's mom.

So rather than run, I handed my baby to the anesthesiologist and fell into my husband's arms and we cried. The anesthesiologist held our baby over his shoulder, and we watched her sweet little crazy-haired head bounce gently up and down as he walked, and she looked back at us, a picture forever etched into my memory. Then the doors closed, and she was gone.

By the time we walked into the downstairs waiting area, the sun had risen. We were greeted by family and social workers and friends, and instead of sadness and fear, an inexplicable and much-appreciated peace wrapped itself around me. What should have been an uncomfortable and scary time was drenched in holiness. I sat in that waiting room, and it hit me: this event was less about my daughter's open-heart surgery and more about having a front-row seat to God's goodness. The thought and the feeling left me breathless.

Isn't that just like our God to surprise us with beauty? Up to this point in my journey, I had seen him take so many seemingly ugly, hurtful, terrifying things and reveal the beauty in them. Again and again and again he had graciously proven his power and faithfulness. On the day of my daughter's open-heart surgery, the day that should have been the darkest and scariest of all, I found my Prince of Peace. All that God had been teaching me about who he was and who he wants me to be was coming together in that hospital waiting area. I had always believed that God uses all things for his glory, but on that day, he showed me. I had never known God as fully as I did then.

All of us have the opportunity to witness these kinds of miracles from the Father, who transforms our fear into hope. For you, the fear may not be rooted in Down syndrome and heart defects. But those miracles are out there, waiting for us to sit down in our front-row seats while God does his thing.

On the cardiac/organ transplant floor was another waiting room lovingly set up by parents who had been in our shoes. The quiet space had soft lighting and comfortable chairs, and a desk with a hospital computer in one corner. A mini fridge had been stocked with snacks and drinks. Encouraging messages were painted on the walls, and booklets full of hope sat on a small table, along with disposable toothbrushes and other travel-size toiletries.

I grabbed a cold bottle of water from the fridge as my parents and Josh each took a seat in one of the comfortable chairs. Soon afterward, Dr. Razzouk came through the door. He was still wearing his scrubs. His kind and humble eyes met ours, and he got straight to the point.

"The surgery went well. I'm glad we got in when we did. Had we waited much longer to close the hole, I'm not sure this surgery would have done much for her." He held up his finger and thumb to make a circle. "I patched up a hole the size of a nickel."

We all gave a little gasp, imagining a hole that large in such a small heart.

The doctor continued. "The next twenty-four hours are critical. I have done all I can do; she is in the Lord's hands. Can I answer any questions for you?"

We should have had a thousand and one questions for the man who had just patched a hole the size of a nickel in our daughter's heart, but the only thing I could manage to ask was, "Is she going to be okay?"

He softly answered, "There are no guarantees. The surgery went well, and she is a strong little girl. As I said before, she is in the Lord's hands."

Josh stood up first and extended his hand. "Thank you so much."

"Can I give you a hug?" My arms were around the surgeon's neck before he could answer. "Thank you for everything. Thank you for saving my daughter's life."

"It is an honor, and I am humbled by people like you who choose to love this little girl."

I stepped back, held my hands to my heart, and simply nodded my head.

A few moments later, a nurse led us to see Macyn. We followed her to the secured wing and watched as she waved her badge over the sensor on the wall. The automatic doors swung open. She repeated Dr. Razzouk's words as we followed her down the hall.

"The next twenty-four hours are critical."

We nodded and tried not to step on her heels.

"During this time, visits can only be ten minutes long. There can only be two people in the room with her, and one of them must be one of you." She stopped outside room 501 and looked us in the face.

"Your daughter is hooked up to a ventilator and lots of other wires and machines. There are two nurses fully committed to her for these next twenty-four hours. She is in the best possible hands."

I tried to peek over her shoulder into the room.

"Can I answer any questions before you go in?"

Josh and I looked at each other and shook our heads.

"Okay then." She moved aside to let us in. "Your daughter is in bed one."

No amount of information could have prepared us for what we saw in that bed. Our daughter was there, but besides her crazy hair, she was difficult to recognize. She was propped up on pillows. Her mouth was open, and out of it came a bumpy tube hooked up to a beeping machine that was helping her breathe. Her eyes were shut and red and swollen from the tape they had used to cover them during surgery. Her left arm was secured by a stiff board and wrapped with a bright yellow sock to protect the IV underneath. Her chest was covered with white gauze, and at the bottom of the gauze near her belly button was a drainage tube, red with the blood and other liquids still needing to drain out of the area that had just been cut open. On the pillow next to her were half a dozen smaller tubes labeled with yellow tape, each one connected to a main line in her neck, each one dispensing a necessary medication to keep her alive during this critical time. Her skin was swollen and red at the places where surgical tape had been removed.

The two nurses assigned to her for the next twenty-four hours, a sassy and cheerful Latino man and a sweet curly-haired woman, were softly communicating with one another, spouting off numbers and words completely foreign to me. They glanced at us as we stood in shock in the doorway and motioned for us to come in, not once losing track of their task at hand.

"She's doing great so far," the nurse with the curly hair told us.

"Can I hold her hand?" I managed to choke out.

"Of course you can," the nurse replied. "We just want to try to keep her sleeping. Rest is important right now."

Josh and I slowly and carefully made our way to the side of her metal hospital bed and gently wrapped her tiny fingers around ours. I looked down at my daughter.

"Hey, sweet girl. Mama's here." I smiled through my tears. "I'm so proud of you. You are doing great. You are going to be fine, my sweet girl." Then I softly sang her the song I had written for her the day she came home to be mine:

> *Who's my little girl with the biggest eyes?*
> *The crazy hair?*
> *The brightest smile?*
> *She's my little one; I love her so much;*
> *I'll love her for ever and ever and ever.*
> *Macyn, Macyn, Macyn Hope, Macyn Hope.*
> *Macyn, Macyn, pretty little Macyn Hope,*
> *Pretty little girl.*

As I sang, my tears landed on her little arm in a puddle of healing love. She began to stir and then grimaced and let out a little cry. Her discomfort was obvious.

"I think it would be best to let her rest." The nurse with the curly hair smiled at us. "You can come back in an hour."

"Okay. Take good care of her." We lingered a little longer and then slowly backed out of her room. As we headed toward the main doors and pushed the button to leave the unit, Josh put his arm around me, and I leaned in and we both cried. Tears of joy for the fact she was alive, tears of shock for what we had just witnessed, and tears of terror over what might happen in the next twenty-four hours.

We spent most of our time in the crowded waiting room down the hall, watching the clock and counting down the seconds until we could spend ten more minutes with our girl. We would walk quickly to her room, always a minute or two early, and walk slowly away, always a minute or two behind. With each passing hour, Macyn became stronger.

The morning after her open-heart surgery, we entered the room during one of our ten-minute visits and found they had taken her ventilator out. She was breathing completely on her own. They also let us know she had been weaned off two of the medications. And one of the night nurses had put Macyn's crazy hair into an adorable ponytail spouting from the top of her head and tied with a tiny red bow. My daughter was looking more and more like my girl. I breathed a little easier.

The next four days were full of beeping machines, little sleep, and the comings and goings of family and friends. On day three, we got to hold her and feed her and whisper in her ear. She was still attached to machines and a mass of cords and tubes, making it slightly terrifying when I would pick her up and a machine began beeping louder and faster because something had come loose. But the nursing staff was pure gold, and they guided us through every tangled tube and upsetting alarm.

I was feeling good. In fact, given the circumstances I was feeling great. I had been thrown into the middle of the ocean and quickly learned I could swim. I dealt with the rip currents and waves like a pro. I was rocking it as a mother with a child in the hospital. This both surprised and pleased me. I was strong enough for this, by God's grace. I was stronger than I ever thought I could be.

Macyn spent a total of four nights in the hospital. As her last night unfolded, the nurses removed all of the tubes and cords except the oxygen tubing. They took the white gauze off her incision, and by morning, she was ready to go home.

We showed up that morning before the sun was up, with Macyn's car seat in hand and a darling little going-home outfit for her to wear. The next few hours were full of discharge instructions and trips to and from the pharmacy to pick up medications. We met one last time with her cardiologist and her surgeon. Both doctors gave us a reassuring thumbs-up and told us to bring Macyn back to see them the following week. A pediatrician came by to answer our questions. She flooded us with pamphlets and information about symptoms to watch for and when to call 9-1-1. Josh and I listened wide-eyed, nodding our heads, trying to pretend we were tracking with her. The strength and confidence I had felt throughout our hospital stay was slowly dwindling.

By early afternoon, all of our discharge tasks had been checked off the list. As we buckled up Macyn, the nurses packed all the extra diapers and bottles and put them in a bag with the stuffed animals and signs that had accumulated in her room during her stay. With thankful hearts, we tightly squeezed the nurses who had been loving on our girl for the past few days. Then we headed to the elevator.

When the sliding door closed, I looked down at my daughter and said out loud over and over, "Thank you, Jesus. Thank you, Jesus. Thank you, Jesus."

Four days ago, I had walked into the hospital thinking I knew my Savior, only to experience his love, goodness, and faithfulness in a way I never knew possible. I was leaving that hospital a changed woman. While Josh carried Macyn in her car seat and I held his hand,

I continued to weep tears of gratitude that God would allow me this opportunity to know him more fully.

When we pulled into our driveway that afternoon, my parents were there with a hot meal. Our fridge was full and our house was spotless. We had set up a bed for Macyn in our room, right next to my bed. Our recovering little girl was asleep when we arrived, so I gently carried her upstairs and laid her in the bed. I checked to make sure her oxygen cannula was secure and kissed her nose, and then I turned on our video monitor and headed back downstairs. We began unpacking the new regimen of medications. Some needed to be refrigerated, and each one needed to be given at a different time, multiple times a day. Josh made a chart so we could track what she had taken and when. I made my way to the kitchen and laid out all the medications and put the syringes in a bowl next to them.

As I headed to the living room to unpack the extra diapers and pull out the signs and stuffed animals, my dad stepped in front of me and gave me a big hug.

"Hey, Elizabeth, you did it. You're home." And at that moment, something in me broke. I had been strong during our time at the hospital. But now that we were home and I didn't have the nursing staff and doctors to keep my daughter alive, I was finding the responsibility of it all more than I could take. I fell into my dad's arms and sobbed.

"I don't know if I can do this. What if I forget a medication or she stops breathing? Dad, what if she dies?" He held me tightly, and I trembled with emotion.

"Heather," he gently replied as he took my shoulders and held me so he could look me in the eyes. "Heather Elizabeth. Every breath she will ever breathe has already been accounted for. Nothing you do or don't do is going to change that. Heather, God's got this. Okay? He's got Macyn, and he's got you."

There it was: life-giving, life-changing truth. We had sat in the hospital in the shadow of death. Now we were home, and that same shadow was knocking on my door, but the truth of my dad's words drowned out the racket that death was trying to make.

The truth my dad spoke that night was branded on my heart. And as the days and weeks and months and years went on, I would say the words out loud whenever I needed to drown out the fear that death would whisper in my ear.

"Every breath she will ever breathe has already been accounted for. Nothing I do or don't do is going to change that."

Pictures and
Letters and So
Much More

When we were nearing our one-year anniversary of bringing Macyn home, we got a call from our social worker. As I answered the phone, I had a feeling I knew what she was about to say.

"Hi, Heather. How are you guys doing? How's Macyn?"

"She's amazing. Things are going really well."

"I'm so glad to hear it." She got right to the point. "I'm calling because Macyn's birth parents contacted us and wanted to see about getting together with you guys. It's been about a year since they last saw you. What are your thoughts?"

Knowing we had given them hope of a once-a-year visit, I knew the answer was yes. But it didn't change the fact that I felt sick to my stomach about it. I had no idea what to expect. *Would they see her and regret their decision? Would they be judging the way we parent? How would their daughter, who is only eighteen months older than Macyn, react to her sister? What would we talk about?*

I pushed all those thoughts aside and said, "Of course we can meet up with them. Can we do it in your office?"

"I think that's a great idea. I'll get in contact with them and set things up." We talked about a good day and time for us, and I hung up the phone full of mixed emotions.

It was a strange, strange feeling to step into a meeting with my child's birth parents. When the day of our visit arrived, Josh and I stood outside the door of the meeting room with our daughter in my arms. And while she was not from my womb, while she was not our blood, she was our daughter in every right. Yet on the other side of the door was a woman I could never compete with: the woman who can look at my daughter and see herself, something I will never be able to do; the woman who cried happy tears when she heard my daughter's heartbeat for the first time, followed by tears of anguish when she decided she could not be the mother Macyn needed. She was the woman who gave my daughter life—and me the opportunity to be a mother.

This was a new space for us. I wasn't sure how to navigate what awaited us beyond the doors.

When we adopted Macyn, we chose to use a private agency. At the time, we were both working and could afford the expensive price tag, but our main reason for going with a private agency was that we thought it would be our ticket to a healthy infant. Also, our research led us to believe our best and safest bet to growing our family as comfortably as possible was through a private agency. Even after all I had learned through my infertility journey about trusting God, I was still trying to grasp as much control as possible. Bad habits are difficult to break, I guess.

The agency we chose required an eight-hour class to prepare us for what lay ahead. During the session, we heard stories from adoptive parents who showed up for their baby's birth, only to find out the birth mother had changed her mind. We heard from foster moms who took babies into their hearts and homes until every *i* was dotted and every *t* crossed and the baby could be placed with adoptive parents. We talked about adoption laws. We were given lists of things to do to make our home safe for our future child. We received stacks of paperwork to fill out. But most of the class time focused on the birth parents.

I had no idea there were so many variables when it came to our future child's birth mother and birth father. Most of us in the classroom that day would be chosen by a birth mother. We would meet her and hopefully the birth father before the baby was born. After the baby was placed in his or her adoptive home, many birth parents hoped to exchange letters and pictures with their child. Some birth families asked for a once-a-year visit in a neutral location. We were told that rarely did birth parents know the last name or address of the adoptive family. Communication between us and our child's birth family would most likely go through the agency.

Then we heard from birth mothers themselves. We watched a video about a young woman who created an adoption plan for her daughter. She looked through binders full of parent profiles. She chose and eventually met the people she hoped would adopt her baby. Years later, she attended her child's birthday party.

On the drive home from our training, Josh and I tried to process this.

"What's your ideal relationship with our future child's birth parents?" I asked him.

He answered without hesitation. "Pictures and letters."

I let out a sigh of relief. "Me too." I picked up our giant adoption binder and began to flip through it. "If I'm being really honest—"

"Nothing has ever stopped you from being really honest," Josh said teasingly.

I gave him a sideways look. "As I was saying, being really honest, I want to pick up my baby and run. I want to be in the room when our baby is born. I want a nurse to hand me the baby. We can give everyone a high five and then throw up some deuces. That's what I really want."

Josh looked at me and smiled. "I hear ya. This whole birth-parent relationship thing feels like an inconvenience."

My hope for future visits with birth parents, or lack thereof, was a reflection of my ignorance at the time. I was looking at this adoption as a way to grow my family, period. While I felt deep, deep gratitude toward our daughter's birth family, I was also steeped in our culture's ideas of what a relationship between an adoptive family and birth family should look like. I was putting my trust in my limited knowledge on the topic rather than in God's best for everyone involved.

I was in for a big surprise.

As we opened the door and stepped into the room with Macyn to visit our daughter's birth parents that first time, all these thoughts swirled around in my head and my heart. Then God gently reminded me of how we had come to this moment in time. The only thing I could do when face-to-face with mystery was hold on to him and his proven faithfulness.

We stepped into the room and my feet walked me straight over to Vickie. "Do you want to hold her?" I asked. When she nodded, I placed Macyn in her arms and draped the oxygen tank over her shoulder. I backed away and found a seat on the black sofa, then breathed in deeply.

Josh walked over to Macyn's three-year-old sister and sat on the floor, picked up the toy next to her, and began pushing the buttons and encouraging her to do the same. With little to no effort, he displayed all the fatherly qualities any parent would want for his child. I watched Josh take on the situation at hand with such ease, and my heart fell in love with him all over again.

Vickie held Macyn and joined me on the couch.

"She's doing good?" she asked in her thick Armenian accent.

"She's doing great!" I reached over and brushed Macyn's hair out of her eyes.

"Can you tell us about the oxygen?" Kaapo asked from a chair across the room.

"Come sit here." I got up from my seat on the couch and ushered him to sit next to Macyn and his wife. "We don't know how long she'll need the oxygen. We go for testing every six months." I took the rocking chair that Kaapo had vacated.

"But it doesn't bother her or limit her abilities much at all," Josh added from his spot on the floor.

As Kaapo and Vickie held Macyn on the couch, I couldn't help but look into their faces and wonder what was going through their minds. My heart began to soften toward them.

"Josh, Heather," Kaapo looked up at us, "we would like to take you to an Armenian lunch. Let's leave from here."

I wanted to shout no! While this meeting was going splendidly, I had come for their sake, not ours. Even though I knew the moment was blanketed in God's goodness, it was still terribly uncomfortable. I wanted to head to the car with Josh and congratulate ourselves on a visit well done.

But before I could come up with a weak excuse, Josh said, "We would love to." He glanced my way to see my reaction.

I gave him a wide-eyed look and then politely smiled at Kaapo. "Sure, I guess that would work."

We followed them to an Armenian restaurant down the street from their home. As we entered, they were greeted familiarly by the people working there, and they exchanged pleasantries in their own language. We sat at a small table near the large window. On the wall above the counter were large photos of plates full of Armenian foods. Some looked familiar, and they reminded me of our time in Romania and Greece; others I didn't recognize.

Kaapo and Vickie proudly asked if they could order for us. Josh and I have always been adventurous eaters, so we were happy for them to choose the foods that would be placed before us that afternoon. As

Kaapo went to the counter to order, Josh pulled two high chairs up to the table and placed them side by side. I pulled out our antibacterial wipes and wiped down Macyn's high chair and the table in front of her. Vickie watched, bewildered.

"We do this all the time." I smiled. "Her lungs are so weak that if she catches even a cold, we could find ourselves in the emergency room." I hoped she understood the words and felt assured she had made the right decision in making me Macyn's mom.

The food began to arrive, and we feasted on roasted veggies and tender meats. We wrapped these up in soft flatbread called lavash and smothered everything in tart hummus. Macyn and her sister sat in their high chairs, and we laughed as they stared each other down. Vickie gasped and apologized when the older girl pulled one of Macyn's pigtails. The language barrier prevented us from having deep and meaningful conversation, but as these birth parents spoke to each other in their native tongue, I felt at peace, knowing we were all doing the best we could. I watched them look at my daughter with such deep love, and I began to love them deeply as well.

As lunch came to a close, we packed up the food left over from our feast, and Kaapo insisted we take it home. Then he said, "Please come to our home for some ice cream. We live only a few blocks away." Josh and I glanced at each other, and this time I spoke up first.

"Thank you so much for the invitation, but we really need to get Macyn home for a nap. It has been a long day for her." I could see the disappointment in their eyes. But not only had it been a long day for Macyn; I selfishly didn't want to be stretched any further. I simply wasn't comfortable with the idea of going to their home. Not yet.

They walked us to our car. Kaapo was quick to open the doors. He gently took Macyn from my arms, and as we loaded up our leftover food and the diaper bag, he and Vickie gently kissed Macyn's soft cheeks. Then he carefully placed Macyn in her car seat and buckled her up.

"Josh, Heather, thank you so much for coming." Vickie said. "Thank you for everything," she whispered with tears in her eyes.

"Yes, thank you," Kaapo chimed in. "Can we get your phone number? We want to see you again, but we like this better than at the agency office. Can we call you and meet up again?"

This request made me feel so uneasy. At this point, I was confident that Macyn's birth parents were good, safe people. I'm a pretty good judge of character and trusted that they were neither psychopaths nor stalkers. But if I gave them our phone number, what then? What if they started to call us every day? What if they used that information to find out where we live? What if they showed up unannounced? What if they wanted us to be a part of their lives? These were the scenarios I hoped to avoid.

Pictures and letters, I thought to myself. All I wanted were pictures and letters.

But in that moment, I also knew I needed to be careful not to let my own comfort get in the way of others' needs. I was reminded that when I'm uncomfortable, I have the chance to know God more fully. So I grabbed a paper and pen and wrote down the ten digits they asked for.

After one more thank-you and a hug good-bye, we headed home, feeling strangely grateful.

Josh broke the silence. "I know this wasn't the relationship we initially hoped for, but they seem so great, so . . . normal."

"I know," I agreed. "I'm having a difficult time letting go of what society has convinced me is the most acceptable relationship with a birth family. I'm wondering if I'm uncomfortable about the idea of a close relationship simply because that's how others would expect me to feel." I looked back at Macyn, who had fallen asleep, and smiled.

"I mean, look at what we get! We're the lucky ones. We get to drive away with this baby as our own. The least we could do is give them our phone number and our time. Right?"

Josh took my hand and nodded. "It's been a crazy journey, and I'm pretty certain it's just beginning."

Months went by, and life went on. Christmas came and went, and a new year started with no word from Macyn's birth parents. My fears of them constantly calling us or showing up unannounced were exposed as unfounded. I was thankful for that, thankful for the normalcy in this anything-but-normal circumstance.

Then in June, a few weeks before Macyn's second birthday, the phone rang.

"Hello, Heather? This is Vickie, Arpi's mom." I knew it was Vickie at *hello*. At the time, she was the only woman in my life with a thick Armenian accent. And she was also the only person who still referred to Macyn as Arpi.

"Vickie," I exclaimed, "so good to hear from you!"

"How is Arpi?" she asked.

"Macyn's doing great," I answered, gently reminding her of the new name. "She's getting big and staying healthy. She'll be two in a few weeks—"

"Heather," Vickie interrupted, "I have a favor to ask."

"Sure, what's up?"

"Kaapo and I would like to give Arpi a birthday party."

That was the last thing I had expected. I could understand them wanting to see her on or around her second birthday, but throw her a party?

"What did you have in mind?"

"We want you and your family to come here for an Armenian barbecue. It will be with my parents and my sisters too. Is that okay?"

Her request seemed perfectly reasonable and completely insane all at once. Never had it crossed my mind that we would meet any of the extended family. But by now, "reasonably insane" seemed to sum up our lives quite well, so I accepted the invitation. She let me know a date she had in mind, and it worked for us.

"What time, and what can we bring?" My mom had raised me right, and I knew better than to show up at an event like this empty-handed.

"Come at ten, and just bring Arpi."

I quickly realized there were some cultural differences in play. In my Western head, we would show up, have some food, hang out, and then head home. But Vickie and her family were extending an invitation for a full-day affair. Though I liked Vickie and Kaapo a lot, spending an entire day with a bunch of strangers who could very well feel entitled to my daughter was not something I was ready for.

"We have church that morning, and then Macyn will need a nap. The best we can do is two o'clock. Will that work?"

"Okay, come at two. I will see you then. Thank you, Heather."

By the time the date rolled around, Vickie and Kaapo had changed the party location from their home to a park because they didn't have enough space in their apartment for everyone. The only person from our side of the family who could join us was my dad, so I wasn't sure who Vickie meant when she said "everyone." Counting her parents and sisters plus our family, I expected fourteen people at the most.

We arrived at a huge park in Glendale right at two o'clock. As we pulled up, I said to Josh, "We just need to look for a large group of Armenians." We got out our lime green umbrella stroller, buckled

Macyn in, and hung her oxygen tank on the stroller handle. Macyn was wearing a multitiered romper, each tier a different pattern of pink and white flowers. She looked as adorable as ever, like a little birthday cake with pigtails.

As we walked from the parking lot, we quickly realized the park was full of large groups of Armenians. It was going to be more challenging than we thought to spot the family we were looking for. We walked down one of the sidewalks and scanned the groups until I spotted a familiar face. Kaapo was walking toward us, waving.

"Hello!" he said. "Come, follow me."

We did as we were told and followed him to a group of picnic tables full of strangers. Vickie ran up to us and gave us all big hugs. "Heather, Josh, thank you for coming!" Her smile revealed heartfelt gratitude and pride.

"Thank you for inviting us. This is my dad, Kim."

My dad, being a hugger like me, embraced Vickie and through tears said, "It is so nice to meet you."

Then Vickie picked up Macyn. I handed her the oxygen bag, and we made our way to the table of faces that were new to us. Vickie introduced us to the family who had come to meet and celebrate our daughter.

There that day were nineteen of Macyn's biological family members. Nineteen! Along with Vickie's parents and three sisters were Kaapo's parents, the brothers-in-law, all of Vickie's nieces and nephews, and a couple of sets of cousins. We exchanged names, and everyone gravitated toward the reason we were all there.

As Vickie and her family spoke loudly and excitedly in a language I did not understand, an epiphany hit me. When Kaapo and Vickie made the decision to create an adoption plan for their child, they were not the only ones to experience a loss. The people there that day lost a granddaughter, a niece, and a cousin—just as our families had gained a granddaughter, niece, and cousin. This life we were living was about so much more than our little nuclear family of three. At that moment in the park, I began to see the beauty that could only be created through the interweaving of our lives with theirs. And I would have missed it all if I had refused to get uncomfortable.

After introductions were made, I sat with the women on the blankets laid out on the grass while Josh and my dad joined the men, who were at the barbecue preparing a feast. Mostly Armenian was spoken, so I spent a lot of the time sitting back, smiling, and trying to read facial expressions. I spent little time worrying about Macyn, because she was more comfortable than any of us and loved all the extra attention. At one point, family members brought over gifts for her, and we spent about thirty minutes opening presents. As Macyn pulled colored tissue paper from bright bags, I was blown away by the love being showered on us. I found myself at times thankful for the language barrier, because I didn't have words beyond "thank you" to express my gratitude.

When the food was ready, we all gathered around the table. Before we ate, one of Vickie's brothers-in-law poured everyone a shot of vodka and held his up for a toast: "To Josh and Heather. We thank you, and we honor you for all you are doing. You are now our family too!" This was followed by loud cheers all around, and everyone threw back their liquor. Then we dug into the feast awaiting us. Huge plates of roasted lamb, barbecued pork, and chicken. Stacks of soft lavash, piles of fresh herbs, bowls full of roasted vegetables, hummus, and olives. Along with a half-dozen bottles of vodka were liters of tarragon-flavored soda and a cooler full of aloe vera juice.

As we all piled the barbecued meats, fresh herbs, and tangy hummus onto soft lavash, the men took turns giving toasts, always honoring

Josh and me, always full of gratitude. From time to time, I would feel someone looking at me and catch the eye of one of the grandparents or aunties. I would smile and think I'd give anything to know what was going on in their heads.

More than once, I caught Vickie's father, my daughter's biological grandfather, looking my way. He had the face of a man whose life had required hard work and sacrifice. I learned he had spent most of his life in Armenia. His eyes were kind and told a story of love for his family. I wanted to get inside his head. I wanted to know what this moment was like for him.

As our time with our daughter's biological family went on, layers of preconceived ideas were peeled away from my heart. If Josh and I had given birth to a child naturally, our lives would have grown by one person. But with this adoption, for better or worse, we would need to make room for more than just our daughter. As I watched these strangers celebrate and love on my girl, God stretched and expanded my heart to include them. This whole time I had believed their loss was our gain, but that day at the park, I began to wonder if their loss could be their gain as well. And maybe my gain would ultimately result in the best kind of loss of all—the loss of my selfish desires.

The sun began to set, and we had a sleepy little girl on our hands. As some of the women in the family began to pack up the leftover food, I laid Macyn down on a blanket and got her into her pajamas. We were ready to leave when Vickie's father came and sat next to Macyn, acknowledging her face-to-face for the first time that day. He smiled at her with his kind eyes, and Macyn stared back at him as he spoke gently to her in his native tongue. I joined them on the blanket. Our eyes met, and I smiled at him.

I pulled Macyn up onto my lap and said, "Macy, can you wave bye-bye and blow him kisses?" She raised her hand and with excitement began to open and close her tiny fingers. Everyone watching laughed out loud. I looked at Vickie's father and said, "I am so sorry, we have to go now." He gave me an understanding nod.

The next few minutes were full of commotion. Family members took turns passing Macyn and her oxygen tank around, careful not to pull on her cannula. I made my way around the crowd, hugging aunties and uncles and cousins. Each expressed their gratitude and said something about how now we were all family.

We were just about to make our exit when I spotted Vickie's father standing a few feet away. I went over to shake his hand, and when I approached him, he gently grabbed me by my shoulders and looked straight at me. I saw he had tears streaming down his face, and my eyes began to well with tears of my own. Then this man, who had only watched me from afar all day, said to me in broken English, "You are like my daughter now." Then he pulled me in for a hug.

We held each other and cried, and I thanked God for pushing me to this place of total discomfort. I thanked God for the grace he had extended to me as he continued to push me away from my own ideas of what is best, ideas that usually involve my security, and toward the blessings I can experience when I die to myself. As I cried in the arms of an old Armenian man, I began to see more clearly how this whole adoption, this whole notion of motherhood and growing a family, was about so much more than just me.

Witness to
a Miracle

In life we often think we know what we want. We do what it takes to get it: flirting with the guy or gal we hope will become our husband or wife; studying and working hard to get into the school or job of our dreams; saving up a little every month to take that big vacation. What we want becomes our goal, and we do everything within our power to make it so.

Then we reach our goals—and oftentimes we discover the guy or gal comes with serious baggage, the school is more difficult than we expected, the new job we worked so hard to attain simply sucks, and hurricane season reduces our vacation to a long hotel-room stay. No matter how hard we work to secure our desires, the unexpected is always waiting for us. The question is not how can we avoid it, but what are we going to do with it?

I once had the goal of becoming a mother. It was all I could think about. I did everything within my power to make it so. And while it came about with twists and turns I desperately tried to avoid, the day came when I met my goal. I held my daughter in my arms.

I was a mother.

But the baby I held in my arms was not the one I had dreamed of. Though her open-heart surgery was successful, her lungs were still terribly sick. When the doctors delivered this news, I looked at my daughter and envisioned a lifetime of oxygen and medication. This was not how I imagined motherhood would look.

I pulled into the Target parking lot and parked in a space closest to a cart-return stall. I grabbed a cart, got out my antibacterial wipes, and wiped down every surface Macyn and I would touch. Then I opened the back door of our SUV.

"Hey, sweet girl!" I smiled at Macyn as she looked at herself in the mirror attached to the backseat. "You ready?" She smiled back at me. I pulled the cart up close to the car and gently slipped Macyn's feet through the holes in the cart seat, careful not to rip the cannula off her face. Then I picked up the green bag that housed her oxygen tank and placed it next to her in the cart.

"There we go." I brushed the hair out of her eyes as she banged her hands on the handle in front of her.

"Mommy," a nearby child said, "what's wrong with that baby's face?"

I looked up to see where the voice was coming from, assuming the child was talking about Macyn, happy to engage in a conversation with the child and his parent.

The mother shushed her son and continued to place bags in the trunk of her car.

I smiled at the boy as we passed by on our way to the entrance of the store.

"But, Mommy, what's on her face?" The child was pointing right at Macyn.

"It's not nice to point," the mother said under her breath as she quickly lifted her child from the cart and placed him into the car.

"It's okay," I began to say, but the mother wouldn't even make eye contact. I looked at Macyn, and we continued inside.

"What's on your face?" I asked her. "The most perfect eyes, nose, and lips I've ever seen!" Macyn giggled and clapped her hands.

We wandered through the baby aisles, picking up diapers, formula, and an irresistible dress on the clearance rack. I noticed every single stare and would simply smile at the people brave enough to make eye contact with me. I wanted to get on the loudspeaker and say,

"Attention, Target shoppers, my baby is on oxygen. You may never have seen a baby on oxygen outside of a hospital until today. No need to stare or point or feel bad for us. And please, if you have any questions, just ask me."

As we waited in the checkout line, a mom with a toddler pulled up behind us.

"Mommy." The toddler pointed at Macyn. "What's in that baby's nose?"

"I don't know, honey." The mom smiled at me. "Why don't we ask her mommy?"

I smiled back, thankful to answer their questions.

Never did I imagine myself pushing a baby in a cart at Target with an oxygen tank nestled in a special bag that hung on my shoulder like a vexing purse of sorts. Nor did I think I would be the mom who would sanitize the baby swing at the park before gently placing my daughter's legs through the holes. I never imagined I would have to push her swing super gently because we were tethered to each other by three feet of tubing.

As time went on, the blisters created by this new pair of shoes slowly began to callous, and what was once an undesired nuisance became my new and almost comfortable normal.

So often in life—and especially in parenthood—we face a massive amount of fear and anxiety about the monsters in the closet. You know what I'm talking about: What if our child doesn't fit into a typical mold? What if *we* don't fit into a typical mold? What are the test results going to say? What might be revealed at the doctor's appointment or the meeting with the specialist? What horrible things might the future hold?

We may find ourselves tucking in our precious children at night or brushing our teeth in front of a mirror, constantly glancing at that metaphorical closet, terrified about what lurks behind the doors. We drop to our knees and pray hard, begging Jesus to spare us from the worst kind of news, the kind that scares us most.

Then, usually after some time has passed, we realize that life has gone on. We've made adjustments, some painful, that have landed us in a new normal. We're making it. Our kid is making it. We're breathing in and out. We're placing one foot in front of the other. We don't think about the monsters as often as we used to. Maybe we've forgotten them completely.

Then one night, as we're tucking our precious child into bed or standing in front of the mirror brushing our teeth, we look over our shoulder at the closet, door slightly cracked, and we slowly walk toward it. As we grab hold of the doorknob, hearing the hinges creak, we wonder what's different, why we now have the courage or curiosity to open it. And with one big brave breath, we quickly swing it open.

The monster we've been fearing this whole time is a red, fuzzy Tickle Me Elmo doll.

We begin to laugh and maybe even cry, because we realize that the monster never had any real power. Our greatest fear, although difficult and life altering, has made us stronger, braver. The monster in the closet hasn't changed. No. *We* have changed.

In spite of our fears for Macyn, Josh and I managed to do life as normally as we could. I confess to occasionally fuming over the nuisance of Macyn's oxygen. More than once, we tripped over the tubing or yanked the cannula out of Macyn's nose when it caught on the arm of a chair. The tape that tore away from her temples would leave a small scratch in its place.

Once, we packed the car and headed to my folks' house for the weekend, only to find upon arrival that we had forgotten to bring Macyn's medication. Skipping a dose could be detrimental to her health, so Josh had to hop back in the car and drive the two-hour round trip to supply Macyn with her life-sustaining elixir.

Our love for travel was stifled because our daughter's lungs could not handle the pressures of an airplane cabin, and our bank account could not afford the necessary equipment to fly with a child on oxygen. Rather than let that get us down, we found alternatives. We took weekend trips to the mountains or the beach. We embarked on eight-hour car rides up the coast to visit family and friends. We even rode a train cross-country to spend a week at my grandmother's farmhouse in Iowa.

While my motherhood role was not unfolding like I had initially hoped it would, I was encountering bits of grace and chunks of joy I would have missed otherwise. Being able to rest fully in God's reassurance that he's got Macyn and he's got me was a new experience. Motherhood is often about scooping up your child and gladly taking the bad with the good because he or she is worth it. Motherhood is about the mingling and intertwining of hearts, which makes it easier to accept the difficult realities, because you will do *anything* for this child of yours.

This was our new normal. Days turned into weeks, weeks into months, and months into years. What once felt like a strange and unwanted reality became a comfortable and, dare I say, enjoyable life unfolding with each new step we took.

Every six months, we would make our way back to the children's hospital to have Macyn's heart and lungs checked. We would walk through the familiar lobby and enter the elevator, reminded of the holy time we spent there. While bouncing Macyn on my lap in the hospital waiting room, I would recall what a privilege it is to sit here knowing that

God's goodness does not hinge on the upcoming procedure or results thereof. I was learning to rest in God's goodness . . . no matter what.

Macyn's routine echocardiograms captured two and three-dimensional images of her heart and detected normal and abnormal blood flow. This procedure showed us how Macyn's heart was functioning and also measured the pressure and blood flow to her lungs, which revealed whether her pulmonary hypertension had changed.

Directly following the forty-five-minute procedure, we would make our way first to the cardiologist, Dr. Kuhn, and then to the pulmonologist. After fitting a couple of these appointments into Macyn's first year with us, Dr. Kuhn told us that as much as he likes our family, he would be seeing less of us. Macyn's repaired heart was beating beautifully, and we could cut our visits back to once a year.

Thank you, Jesus! Oh that you would be glorified with every single beat.

Her lungs, on the other hand, were not getting stronger. With each visit to pulmonology, we would enter the doctor's office with our fingers crossed and hold our breath until the doctor joined us in the tiny white room.

Our pulmonologist was Dr. Fanous. She was as sassy as she was brilliant. The first time we met, my husband asked her about her thick, beautiful accent, and she told us she was from Egypt.

My husband replied, "My college mentor has the last name Fanous, and he's also Egyptian. I know it's a long shot, but do you know a John Fanous? He lives in the San Francisco area and works with InterVarsity at SFSU."

"He's my nephew," she replied with a sly grin. We viewed this connection as another example of God's favor over our daughter. I had prayed for favorable relationships with the medical professionals in Macyn's life. My hope was that God would grant us a way to be more than just another face in the doctors' offices. In this season of cannulas and concentrators, the ties between us and the Fanouses was like a wink from God giving us that extra peace we needed.

Our first appointment with Dr. Fanous was in December 2008, shortly after Macyn's surgery. With six months between every visit, we would always find ourselves in her office at the beginning of the Christmas season and at the start of summer. Unfortunately, the appointments became a familiar scene. We would show up at Dr. Fanous's office with the results of Macyn's echocardiogram; Dr. Fanous would read the results; she would say to us, "Your daughter's pulmonary hypertension is still there. We will see her in six months."

Our hearts would sink slightly as we gathered up our daughter and her oxygen tank.

But on December 15, 2010, things took a life-altering turn.

"What do you want me to do with these mint bars?" Josh yelled from the kitchen.

"Just cover the platter with foil." I turned the corner into the kitchen with Macyn on my hip.

"What else can we do beforehand?" We were headed to our six-month appointment with Dr. Fanous, and afterward we would host a Christmas party for Josh's staff. We had little time between the appointment and the party, so we were hustling around trying to get everything done.

"Honestly, not much." I looked at the list on the counter. "All the appetizers are in the freezer, ready for a 400-degree oven. Cookies and sweets are on platters." I glanced at the decorated table and bar area.

"We just need to grab some ice for the bar on our way home. Besides that, we're set."

Josh looked at the clock on the wall. "We gotta go." I handed him Macyn and grabbed the diaper bag, and we headed for the car.

I knew about Macyn's appointment when I agreed to host this Christmas event. I didn't think much of it. All that was needed was a little planning.

Macyn had her echocardiogram done the day before our appointment with her pulmonologist, so we headed straight to Dr. Fanous's office. We pulled into the parking lot of the specialty clinic; unbuckled our sweet girl; adjusted her cannula, which she had pulled out of her nose; grabbed her oxygen tank; and made our way to the second floor. We checked her in, shared pleasantries with the staff behind the counter, and sat down to wait for the nurse to call our name.

We made eye contact with the other parents in the waiting area, parents living in a reality they probably never would have chosen for themselves or their child. With one smile, we could quickly figure out who had opened the closet door and discovered the Elmo doll, and who still worried about the monsters it contained. Some engaged in conversation. Others averted their eyes, maybe because they simply wanted to get through their child's appointment without having to talk to anyone but a doctor.

We read a few books and ate a few snacks, and then a nurse came. "Macyn?"

We gathered our things and walked her way.

"Hi, guys. How are you doing today?"

"We're great," I said. Macyn clapped and babbled in agreement.

We followed the nurse through the door and down the hall, Macyn on my hip and her oxygen tank securely in a bag hanging over my shoulder. The nurse proceeded to weigh and measure her, check her temperature, take her blood pressure, and wheel over the pulse-ox machine and wrap a tiny sensor on her big toe to measure her oxygen levels. We watched the number rise to 97, 98, 99, and finally 100, which is to be expected for a baby on oxygen. The reading on this tiny device held the key to Macyn's freedom. She would need to stay above 97 on her own in order to proceed with an oxygen-free life.

After the nurse gathered the necessary information, we followed her to one of the many tiny exam rooms and waited for Dr. Fanous. Macyn reached for the paper-covered table and started giggling as she crinkled, shredded, and tried to eat the thin and apparently delicious stuff.

"It's going to be tight," Josh said as he looked at the clock. "What needs to happen when we get home?"

"Well, we need to stop for ice and cook all the apps. Really, not that much—"

We were in the middle of a sentence when Dr. Fanous opened the door and announced in her beautiful, thick Egyptian accent, "Her pulmonary hypertension is gone. Take off her oxygen!"

Josh and I just sat there, silent, stunned.

"I said it is gone. Take off her oxygen," demanded our sassy and wonderful doctor.

"Wait, what?" Josh and I looked at each other and began to cheer and sob. We wrapped our arms around each other, Macyn between us, and jumped up and down in joy.

"I don't understand," Josh said as I gently pulled the tape off Macyn's soft and slightly scabbed cheeks and took the obnoxious cannula out of her nose as I'd been commanded to do.

"Well," Dr. Fanous started to explain, "her levels in her last echo came back normal. What we need to do now is take her off oxygen, and in thirty minutes we will measure her pulse-ox levels to see how she does. If she can stay above 97, we will send you home oxygen-free."

"Really?" I asked in a tearful whisper.

"Really!" Dr. Fanous smiled at me. "Her pulmonary hypertension is gone."

I picked up my oxygen-free girl, held her cheek against mine, and spun her around and around, something I could never have done when she was attached to her tank. We laughed. I had dreamed of this moment for more than two years but never really knew if it would come.

Having a baby with an incurable and possibly life-shortening disease is never on a mother's list of desires for her child. But in that moment when I spun around the doctor's office with my oxygen-free daughter, I couldn't believe my luck. It had been a difficult road, yes. But with each twist, turn, and pothole, I gained a patient strength. I learned that God's goodness and faithfulness do not hinge on my daughter's health, yet this same goodness was extended to us when God gave us Macyn, and then gave us this moment.

With each past disappointing echocardiogram, with each stumble over the stupid oxygen tubing, with each night spent praying the line wouldn't find its way around my daughter's neck and choke her, all I could do was lean more and more into the strength of my Jesus. As I held my daughter that day in the doctor's office, tossing her up in the air and spinning her around, waiting for the thirty minutes to pass, I felt so lucky that I got to be the one to witness this kind of miracle. I felt myself lean into Jesus again, but this time not for strength. I leaned in because I didn't know any other way to show him the gratitude I felt.

Thirty minutes ticked by, and the nurse showed up again with the pulse-ox machine and strapped the sensor around Macyn's big toe. We held our breath as the numbers flashed and began to rise slowly until they consistently teetered between 97 and 98.

"She's good to go, guys," Dr. Fanous announced.

I was still stunned by this unexpected miracle. "So we just go?"

"Yes. Continue with the medication and keep her on oxygen at night for now. Her body doesn't know life without them, so we will need to wean her off."

Josh and I nodded while Macyn played with the tiny light on the pulse-ox machine.

"Come back in three months, and we can reevaluate and adjust as needed. Okay?" She looked at us, and we continued to nod. "Now go, get out of here. I only see sick babies; your baby is not sick." She gave us her sly grin.

"Dr. Fanous, can I hug you?" My arms were around her neck before she could answer. "Thank you so much. Thank you!" I whispered as she hugged me back.

A small crowd of nurses and staff gathered around our little circle of joyous commotion in the hall. "It's gone! Our daughter is healed!" I announced to anyone who would listen and passed out hugs to everyone within reach.

As soon as we walked outside, I was on my phone. "Mom, guess what!" I cried all over again as I proceeded to tell her every detail of the holy moment we had just experienced.

"Wait a second, Heather," she interrupted. "Let me get your father on the phone . . . Kim!" she yelled, and I heard another line pick up.

"Hey, Dad, she's healed. Her pulmonary hypertension is gone." The three of us cheered and laughed and cried as I made a scene in the parking lot.

As we drove home, we took turns making phone calls to our family. I sent text messages to the dozens of people who had been on this journey with us. Many of the texts were followed by calls from my friends, who cried when I confirmed they had read my message right.

"Yes!" I would exclaim. "It's really gone. She's in her car seat right now with *no* oxygen!" Then there would be more laughing and more tears.

We pulled up to the house just as the sun was going down. Josh grabbed Macyn out of the car, and before we went inside to prepare for our party guests, we stopped and looked at our daughter. We both kissed her and took a deep breath.

"Babe," Josh said as he grabbed my hand, "it's gone."

More than two years ago, Josh had held my hand in this same spot and reassured me we were making the right decision to bring this baby into our lives. Now I just smiled and nodded and stood there speechless. Then Macyn reached for me. I held her and looked at Josh.

"Okay, we've got a party to throw and so much to celebrate. Let's go inside." We returned to our home much different people than we had been when we left.

Arms Wide Open

Josh and I started the adoption process for Avis baby number two when Macyn was two years old.

This second time around was so much different from the first, and I would guess this is the case for women who grow their families naturally as well. I imagine being pregnant while raising a toddler is a whole different ball game from being pregnant without one.

But the difference for me between our first adoption and our second had nothing to do with the tasks and everything to do with my heart. Man oh man, had God done a work in my heart.

When we started the adoption process the first time, I was pretty sure I knew exactly what I needed. I wanted a healthy infant and did everything in my power to make my desires come to fruition. Then God gave me Macyn—a sick baby girl with Down syndrome. Two years later, when we began the process for our second adoption, God had shown me how his best for me was nothing I could have planned. Macyn had rocked my world and opened my eyes to the beauty and joy I wouldn't have seen otherwise.

So with this second adoption, I sat before the Lord with arms wide open and said, "God, I will adopt any child you send my way."

Being wide open for our next adoption changed everything. For starters, we chose to adopt through the county instead of a private adoption agency. We knew the risks this involved. For example, we knew that the majority of babies adopted through the county have been exposed to drugs in utero. But we were up for the challenge, believing that God is bigger than "incurable" lung diseases and bigger than an addiction to methamphetamines. Plus, the cost for a county adoption in our area is zero dollars. That's right, it's totally free. Because I had been a stay-at-home mom for the past two and a half years, it was the right kind of price.

Our local county adoption began with a "taking care of business" day. On this day, prospective adoptive and foster parents attend an orientation, are fingerprinted, are given a TB test, and fill out the first of a million forms.

At the orientation, we learned we would have to complete twenty-four hours of classes. We would need to update our CPR and have a new home study done. We were told it was highly unlikely we would get a baby and basically impossible to get a healthy baby.

As the social workers stood on the stage instructing us, I felt the nerves in my gut start to churn. The idea of saying yes to *any* child this time around was beginning to sound crazy. God had been doing a grand work in me, and I had surrendered most of my desires to him, but in times like these, I was still prone to seek comfort by reaching for something I could control.

As we walked to the car, Josh took my hand and said, "This is crazy. It is so different from how things went with the private agency."

"Right! That felt like the Ritz. Now we're sleeping at a Motel 6."

Josh pulled up a picture of Macyn on his phone. "But look at this. She's our first end result. God's got something great, I just know it." Josh gave my hand a reassuring squeeze, and we headed home to give Macyn a big hug and kiss.

The next few months were full of all things adoption. We began filling out the paperwork, leaving nothing about ourselves to be assumed. With each form I filled out, I would pray for our future child. As I wrote my address for the hundredth time, I would think about that child's tiny feet running around our home.

It was a wild thing to think that our child had already been conceived, maybe even born. That his or her little heart was beating in another woman's womb as tiny fingers and little ears were forming. I thought about God's good and perfect plan for my life. I pondered the mystery of one woman's grief being my joy. I thought about these things and stepped into this adoption with a reverence for brokenness that I was lacking the first time around.

A year later, on August 26, 2011, I was frantically running around the house putting things together for a party my husband was having at work. I had Macyn in her high chair with small bites of soft tofu and tiny squares of roasted butternut squash on her tray. I was grabbing sippy cups and diapers and shoving them into our diaper bag.

I had volunteered to help my friend who was hosting the party, and I didn't want to be late. I had just grabbed a wet washcloth and was wiping off Macyn's messy hands when our phone rang. I almost let the answering machine pick it up, but it was sitting right next to me, so I glanced at the caller ID. "Private Caller," it read, and my stomach dropped.

"Oh my word, Macyn, this is it." I looked at my daughter. "This is the call." I set down the washcloth and wiped my hands on my dress. Clearing my throat, I answered. "Hello?"

"Hi, Heather, it's Katie." Katie was our semiretired social worker, who worked a few cases as the county needed her. We were so blessed to be assigned to Katie. At our first meeting with her, I was disappointed that she lacked the warmth I'm usually drawn to in a person. But she was good at her job—exceptionally good. I trusted her expertise and her ability to get our family matched with the right child.

"We have a child for you," she said.

When I first heard her voice that day, I thought she sounded too calm to be delivering news about a child. But that was Katie. She was always steady, a welcome anchor for Josh and me in what was sometimes a tumultuous process.

At her words, my mama heart—the heart that didn't know how it could love another child like it loved my Macyn—expanded to twice its size. For me, the love I felt was instantaneous, and I didn't even know if it was for a boy or a girl.

"Really?" I squealed.

Katie continued in businesslike fashion. "We have a little girl for you. She's five months old. Her birth mom is Guatemalan, and the birth dad is unknown. She has no major health concerns we can see at this time. She was placed in a loving foster home straight from the hospital and has been doing wonderfully with them. What do you think?"

What did I think? What did I think! Oh my, so many things. But I said, "Katie, I need her. She sounds perfect. What do we do now?"

"First there will be a meeting with you and Josh, me, the baby's social worker, and a team of other social workers," Katie began to explain. "During this meeting, we'll give you all the information we have on the baby, including a picture."

"I seriously have to wait for a picture?"

"This is a mandatory meeting, and I can't tell you anything more about the baby until then."

"But I want her now, Katie."

"You'll have to wait." There would be no rule bending, no funny business.

"Okay, I guess I'll do as you say!" I said with a tease.

"The ball is rolling; she'll be in your arms soon."

"I can't wait. Thank you, Katie!"

I called Josh at work.

"We're getting a baby!" I shouted, and I jumped up and down in the kitchen, doing a little celebration dance while Macyn waved her hands in the air and laughed at my antics.

"Wait, what?" He was stunned. "Tell me what you know."

"All I know is she's a five-month-old girl who is half Guatemalan."

"A daughter!" His voice cracked, and I knew he was crying.

"Hey, I'm headed your way, so I'll give you all the details then. I'm running super late; I've got to jet."

"Heather, wait," he shouted before I could hang up. "She's our Truly? She's our Truly Star, right?"

We had loved the name Truly for a while now, and my older sister's middle name is Star, but we had never said it out loud like this, like bringing a real-live child into existence, into our family.

"Yes! We finally have our Truly Star."

Our county's department of children and family services was located in what used to be a mall. Most of the old storefronts were full of cubicles and fax machines. What were once a Hallmark store and women's clothing store were now meeting areas with large oval tables surrounded by chairs. We had taken most of our required classes in these rooms, so it was a familiar space for us. Still, the county offices can be a strange and mostly uncomfortable place for any parent.

We arrived early and walked through the sliding doors. More common than adoptive parents walking through those doors were parents who have had their children removed from them. As we waited for our social worker, we watched parents arrive and tell the person working behind the counter that they had come for a visit. Then foster parents came in, holding babies or the hands of young children. We watched school-age children quickly drop the hand of their foster parent and run into the arms of their mom or dad. We watched babies as they were pried out of their foster parent's arms and placed in the arms of their mother—a stranger. We watched toddlers cry into the shoulder of their social worker or foster parent when they were told their mom or dad didn't show up.

I grabbed tightly to Josh's hand and wiped tears from my eyes, mystified by and angry at this "system" we were now a part of. I was reminded of the initial tragedy that had to take place for me to be there. In our case, a woman was not able to parent her daughter, and a critical relationship was severed before the sun set on Truly's first day of life.

Silently I pleaded with God to heal the brokenness present in that space. I found my heart breaking equally for the innocent child stuck in the negative repercussions of his or her parents' choices, and for the parents who were also stuck, often unable to escape difficult circumstances. Brokenness upon brokenness.

When Katie arrived and asked us to follow her to the room where we would joyously learn about our new daughter, I was thankful to have witnessed the events in the waiting area. It was important for me to understand that when I said yes and followed God into these new relationships, I was also saying yes to brokenness, to pain, to surrender—and to knowing the grace of God more fully.

We walked into a stark room and sat down in the two empty chairs at the long rectangular table. Sitting across from us were three county workers: the birth mother's social worker, our new adoption placement social worker, and Katie. In front of them were manila folders, notepads, and pens. I got out my notepad and a pen and wiped my clammy hands on my jeans.

Katie asked, "So how are you guys feeling?"

"Great," Josh said. "We're anxious to learn more about this baby."

I resisted the urge to nervously bite my nails.

"Let me start with what the next steps will look like." Katie was best with these practical details. "At this meeting, we will tell you everything we know about the baby. You can ask us any questions you may have, and we'll answer them if we can. You'll then have a mandatory twenty-four-hour period to decide whether or not you want to adopt her. If you say yes, then we'll set up visits for you at the foster home. Because she is five months old and has been in the same foster home the whole time, we will schedule a few days of visits before she goes home to you."

So far so good, I thought as I listened. Except for the twenty-four-hour thing, and the slow transition. I wanted my daughter *now.* It didn't matter what they might tell me about her; she had already managed to enter my heart, and I loved her. I felt as though I needed her that very second. But I knew the rules and was not surprised at how things would need to unfold. I had to go along with it, but I didn't have to like it.

The birth mother's social worker went on to tell us everything she knew about the birth mom. She was born and raised in Guatemala, and then she went to college in Mexico City before finding her way to California. We were told she was articulate, fair-skinned, and petite. Parts of her story felt heavy and terrifying. Elements of it could affect our daughter's future in unknown, scary ways.

As I listened, I found myself once again on a roller coaster, holding on tight and trying not to puke. I was ready for this baby and everything she brought with her. If I had learned one lesson by this time, it was that I should stop worrying about the future. God had proven himself time and time again. Old habits die hard, though. I would try to avoid the scariest unknowns if I could.

But parenthood and adoption exist smack-dab in the center of

Unknownville. I remembered this as I looked across the table at these three people who held the latest key to my family's growth. Just as I was about to excuse myself for some fresh air, God showered his grace on us.

Our social worker asked, "Do you want to see a picture?"

Her inquiry pulled me off the nauseating roller coaster and back to reality. *Wait? What?*

"Yes!" Josh and I practically shouted.

Then there she was, our Truly Star, a little slice of heaven on Kodak paper.

The room became silent as all three social workers looked at us with big smiles. We looked at her picture with tears in our eyes, huge grins on our faces, and my hand clutching my heart.

The baby staring back at us from that photo was gorgeous—not in the new-baby way, but in the way that extends past a parent's eyes and crosses cultural ideas of the word. Her image knocked the breath out of me. I looked at her deep-set, dark brown eyes. The expression on her face was serious and gave her an old-soul aura. Her skin was the most perfect shade of brown, almost the color of cinnamon, but even more delicious. Her nose sat perfectly in the center of her face. Her lips were closed and looked like a sweet little bow. And her cheeks—oh those cheeks! They were begging for me to kiss them a million times each. Her head was covered in silky black hair and adorned with a huge pink flower bow. She was lying on her back, and her hands were folded across her tummy. Her body language made it feel as though she was lying there waiting for me, waiting for her mommy to call her, *child*.

She was perfect! She was more than I could have hoped for. And I loved her so much already.

After staring at her for what felt like an hour but in reality was just minutes, Josh said, "She's so beautiful." His voice cracked.

"She really is such a pretty baby," one of the social workers agreed, and they all nodded.

I spoke up. "I need her. So what now?"

Katie reminded us of the mandatory twenty-four-hour "sleep on it" phase.

I held in my hand a photo of my daughter—my heart-pumping, lungs-expanding, living-and-breathing daughter—knowing I would have to wait a whole week or longer before I could breathe her in and kiss those chunky cheeks. I wanted her that very minute.

The emotion in my gut wanted to protest and demand I get my baby *now*! But my rational self, combined with our experiences so far, simply looked my social worker in the eye and said, "Okay. We'll be calling you tomorrow."

We shook everyone's hands, thanked them for their time, and left the office holding tightly to each other as we stared at the photo of our daughter.

We watched the clock and counted the minutes as we waited for twenty-four hours to pass, and as soon as it did, we placed the call and gave our official yes. Katie set up the necessary visits with the foster family, and before we knew it, the day arrived when we got to bring Truly Star home.

When we went to her foster home to pick her up, we found ourselves once again entangled in the mystery of joy and sorrow so perfectly interwoven. Everyone in her foster family was there taking turns holding her and giving her kisses. They remained positive and strong, and though Truly was one of dozens of children they had fostered and placed into the arms of loving parents, I knew this day was sad for them. They had spent almost six months with this precious baby girl, loving her as their own.

We finished loading up the car with the few items belonging to Truly. Her foster mom gave her one last kiss and placed her in my arms.

"There is no way I could ever thank you enough," I told her. "You have been the mama our little girl needed, and you've shown her so much love. Thank you! We have your number, and I promise we'll keep in contact."

She gave me a tearful smile. We hugged her, and then Josh buckled Truly into her car seat, and we drove off.

Boom—we were officially a family of four.

We pulled up to our house. In the short time we were away, my creative and thoughtful mom had put up a big banner welcoming Truly Star home. Hana's car was in the driveway. My younger sister had come from Los Angeles to be with us on this exciting day and to meet her new niece for the first time. My sister Harmony and her youngest, Addison, had made an eight-hour drive to meet Truly.

We pulled into the garage and opened the back door of the car to find Truly sound asleep. Josh gently lifted the car seat out as I walked in first and was met by the beaming faces of my parents and sisters.

"Shh," I quietly said, "she's fast asleep."

Josh set the car seat on the floor as we all gathered around Truly and watched her sleep.

Harmony grabbed my hand. "Heather, she's so gorgeous."

"I know, right?"

"But *really*," Hana chimed in, "she's a total babe."

Macyn was sitting on the floor next to me, and I scooped her up into my lap. "Hi, big sister." I kissed her on the head. "What do you think of your new little sis?"

Macyn's sappy grin spoke the words she didn't know how to say yet.

"Baby?" She pointed at Truly and looked at me.

"Yes, Macy, that's our new baby. Do you love her?"

"Mm-hmm." She responded with the same googly look everyone in the room shared at that moment.

Truly began to stir. We all gave our own quiet little gasp, and then the whole room held its breath while her eyes began to open. Josh and I leaned in closer to her.

"Hey, sweet girl," I whispered, "welcome home."

9

Love in Action

Girlfriend, you cannot wear that today." I was in the kitchen making scrambled eggs when four-year-old Truly came down the stairs.

"But, Mommy!" our second daughter whined.

"Truly, it's super cold out today."

"But look at it twirl!" Truly gave a spin, and the light summer dress flared at the bottom.

"Sweetie, it's wintertime. You may *not* wear that dress." I grabbed plates from the cupboard and began to divvy up the eggs.

"But, Mommy, I'll wear a sweater and tights."

"Truly, please don't argue with me." I stopped what I was doing in the kitchen and got on my knees, eye to eye with Truly. "We have this conversation almost every day, sweetheart. You know better."

"But, *Mommy*!" Truly's shoulders slouched, and her voice went up ten octaves.

"Truly, do not argue. Please go upstairs and put on something warm."

"Fine!" She stomped upstairs with the sass and finesse of a sixteen-year-old drama queen.

"And change your attitude, young lady." I shouted to her as she walked away. Then I mumbled under my breath, "Dear Jesus, full of mercy and grace, I'm gonna need a little extra."

This scene was repeated numerous times as Truly continued to come downstairs in dresses that were either too summery or too fancy for preschool, until I finally went upstairs and pulled out an appropriate choice, which she was opposed to. Of course.

These disagreements about almost everything in life—what she'd wear, what she'd listen to, how she walked (or rather, jumped, skipped, crawled, rolled, scooted) from point A to point B—seemed to follow Truly and me throughout our days. This tension showed up quite soon after she joined our family, and it rocked my world as a mother. Remember that work God had done in my heart through our adoption of Macyn? He wasn't finished with me yet.

Let me take you back a bit.

I stood in a dimly lit room at the back of our church sanctuary, often referred to as the "mothers' room." I cradled Truly and shushed her to the rhythm of my bouncing. "Shh, shh, shhhhh. Shh, shh, shhhhh." My mantra should have helped her fall asleep. Truly looked up at me with her big sparkly brown eyes, wide-awake.

"Truly, you need to go to sleep," I whispered softly to her. She wiggled in my arms and tried to sit up. I held her tighter and bounced higher and shushed louder. And I began to feel it bubble inside of me: extreme annoyance.

Within weeks of Truly coming home, this feeling of annoyance started raising its nasty head whenever she would refuse to let me feed her or would fight me when I tried to dress her. The irritation was something I had not felt before, not like this, and I hated it.

"SHH, SHH, SHHHH!" I made the sound through gritted teeth. "Just go to sleep." I held her even tighter. Still, she just looked at me with those beautiful eyes, wriggling to get out of my almost-too-tight grip. She did not want to comply. I felt all kinds of negative feelings toward her as I continued my bouncing and my shushing until finally her eyes got heavy, and she fell asleep.

I was the only mother in there that morning, and I slowly made my way to one of the five empty rocking chairs along the back wall.

I gently sat down, my arms cramping because I didn't want to jostle her and wake her up. The small speaker in the corner of the room was softly pumping in the sermon, but I wasn't paying attention. I sat there, staring at my sweet, innocent daughter asleep in my arms. My feelings of annoyance instantly turned to guilt.

She's just a baby, I thought to myself. Why couldn't I just let her stay awake? Why did I insist she fall asleep? Why do I feel such irritation?

I convinced myself she wasn't aware that the harder bouncing and louder shushing were actions born from negative feelings. I told myself I wouldn't let it happen again.

But I knew something was different this time around. Josh and I had decided to keep Truly out of the nursery because church happened to fall right during naptime. The deeper reason was that I didn't want a sweet nursery worker to bond with Truly when she and I were still far from bonded. The truth was, this adoption was not unfolding like I had hoped it would.

During those first few months after we brought Truly home, everything felt new and exciting. Macyn embraced her role as a big sister, and she and Truly seemed to become instant best friends. Truly was a happy baby and a good sleeper. When we went out in public or spent time with friends, Truly quickly owned her middle name, Star, and made herself the star of the hour. Her undeniable beauty paired with her charm made her a crowd favorite.

So it's not surprising that I didn't notice right away, especially in those first few months, that my feelings toward Truly were not what I wanted them to be. As time went on and the newness of our relationship faded, an ugliness in my heart began to surface.

As parents, we can only do what we know while continuing to learn. What I knew about being a mom was all wrapped up in Macyn. When Macyn came home, she made me a mother and filled my aching void. She needed me just as much as I needed her. Not only did she need my help to sit, crawl, eat, and walk; for those first couple of years, she needed me for her very survival. These realities helped us bond from the second she was in my arms. It's embarrassing to admit, but as a recovering control freak, I liked how much she needed me.

Enter Truly Star. Apart from the practical care she needed as a baby, Truly was Miss Independent from the second she entered our lives. She was able to sit, crawl, eat, and walk without one session of therapy or extra assistance from me. She was more curious than any child I had ever met. It was as though she was constantly looking to Josh and me to show her where the line was, just so she could cross it. She also happened to be the most energetic kid I had ever met, bouncing off the walls from the second she woke up until the time her head hit the pillow at night.

"She sounds like a pretty normal kid, Heather," my sister Harmony would say when I'd call to vent about Truly's actions for the day. "I think you're just used to Macyn."

"No, Harmony," I'd explain, often through tears of frustration. "I've been around lots of other kids besides Macyn. Truly has excessive amounts of energy, spunk, and attitude."

When Truly was about a year old, we went to visit Harmony and her family.

"Okay," Harmony yelled after me as I chased Truly out the front door. My daughter had outwitted the child safety lock and was on her way to the yard. "You were right. She's not like other kids."

The validation was nice, but it didn't fix the problem. Because the problem wasn't with Truly; the problem was with me.

I realized I had put unfair and unrealistic expectations on Truly and then resented her for not meeting them. I expected her to be a tiny bit compliant. I expected her to need me. I expected her to allow me to be in control, not to want it for herself. As a mom, I could not figure out how to put age-appropriate boundaries around Truly's zeal for life, desire for independence, and immeasurable curiosity. In all honesty, these traits significantly challenged my need for control. After an especially challenging day, I'd find myself lying in bed, looking into the darkness, fearing I was taking Truly's God-given gifts and squelching them.

When Truly was smack-dab in the middle of her terrible twos, we took a day trip to my parents' house. It was the end of summer, and the temperature was expected to hit the triple digits. Josh was working, and the thought of being stuck in the house all day with two toddlers was suffocating me. So I packed up our car and headed to the local mountains, where I could expect it to be at least fifteen degrees cooler.

"Gum, Mama!" Truly demanded from her car seat.

"Tru, you swallowed your last piece, so you don't get any more today."

"GUM!" she screamed at me.

"No." My reply was calm, but I could feel my blood start to boil. I turned up the music to drown out her cries.

By the time we wound our way up the mountain, she had forgotten about the gum. We pulled up to my parents' house. The cool breeze blowing through the blanket of green forest affirmed my decision to leave the heat.

"Hi, guys!" my mom yelled from the large deck as my dad made his way down the steep steps toward the car.

"Papa!" Truly ran from the car into my dad's arms.

"Hi, Tru Star." My dad scooped her up.

"Honey-gram!" Macyn sat on my hip and pointed to my mom.

We headed up the steps and joined my mom on the deck. My dad set Truly down, and I put Macyn on the porch swing.

"Tru, no!" I ran and steadied the flowerpot she was about to pull down. "Truly, you cannot pull these down. You can look at the flowers and smell the flowers, but you cannot pull them down." The explanation was pointless, as Tru was already making her way into the house. I stopped her as she reached on her tiptoes for the handle on the screen door.

I held the door shut. "We're going to stay outside for a little bit." Truly again reached for the handle and tried to open the door. "Tru, we're staying outside." She gave me a sideways glance as if to say, *You say I can't go inside? Just watch me!* and proceeded to try to open the door again. I held it shut.

"NOOOOOO! INSIDE!" she screamed. I picked her up, and she began to flail.

"Let's go sit on the swing with Macy and Honey-gram." She seemed to like this idea and calmed down a bit—for as long as it took the seat to swing back and forth twice.

"Gum, Honey-gram?" Truly asked sweetly.

"Truly, we talked about this. No gum," I answered before my mom could.

From my daughter's reaction, you might have thought I said I was going to throw her from the deck onto the street below.

"Come on, Heather, she can have some gum." My mom gave me a look.

"Seriously, Mom?"

I picked Truly up as she sobbed dramatically. "Hooooney-gram! I want Honey-gram!"

I gave my mom a stern you-better-butt-out-of-this look and took Truly into the house.

"Truly, it is not okay to behave this way. You are going to sit in time-out for two minutes."

"No!" Truly's sobs increased. I set a timer. She screamed.

Our day at my parents' house proceeded in this fashion. She filled the next few hours with fits, sneaky behavior, persistent dramatic sobbing, manipulation, defiance, and more. I noticed the looks on my parents' faces when I set Truly down for her millionth time-out.

"I'm open to suggestions."

"Heather, you're doing a great job." My mom came over and put her arm around me, and we both collapsed on the couch.

"I feel like I'm working so hard for nothing." I buried my head in my hands and began to cry. "It'd be one thing if I didn't discipline and guide and correct her and she acted this way. But I'm working my butt off, and she's still out of control."

"She's not out of control, Heather," my dad said, joining us on the couch. "She's got a lot of energy, and she wants to figure things out on her own, and she's only two. She's a handful."

Our conversation was interrupted by a crash in the other room. I ran to discover that Truly had gotten out of her time-out chair, climbed onto the bed, pulled the lamp down, and broke it.

"What in the world?" I picked her up, moved her away from the broken glass, and handed her to my dad. My mom brought a trash can over, and we began placing the big chunks of glass inside. "I'm sorry, Mom."

"Don't be silly, Heather. It's just a lamp."

"Dad," I yelled after him, "will you put the girls' shoes on? We're going to go."

"You don't have to leave."

"I know. But I need to. I'm sorry."

We packed up our stuff and headed to the car.

"Thanks for having us." I gave my dad a hug. "Sorry if we ruined what could have been a relaxing day."

My dad finished buckling Macyn into her car seat.

"Elizabeth, you did not ruin anyone's day, so don't talk like that."

I shrugged my shoulders and got into the driver's seat. I closed the door and rolled down the windows.

"Wave good-bye to Honey-gram and Grandpa." The girls and I all waved.

"Heather," my dad called after me as I backed down the steep driveway, "don't grow weary in doing the right thing."

I gave him a weak smile and drove away.

During the drive home, I was all wound up and fuming. I blasted kids' music in the rear speakers until the girls both fell asleep, and then I turned the music off, happy for some silence.

The right thing? I thought about what my dad had said. The problem was, I had no idea whether or not I was doing the right thing in raising Truly. No idea.

I looked in my rearview mirror at my daughters asleep in the backseat. *What is my deal? I'm ruining her. I just know it.* I hated myself for having these thoughts. I hated that when I looked at my sleeping daughter, I felt more frustration than warm fuzzies. I wondered if my lack of emotional connection was an adoption thing. I doubted I would feel this way had I given birth to Truly.

I needed someone to tell me she was going to be okay, that I wasn't going to ruin her. Or better yet, someone to tell me exactly what to do.

The next day, I met up with my "village" for coffee. My village consists of five other moms. We found ourselves doing life together after I read the book *Bread & Wine* by the ever-so-lovely Shauna Niequist. The second I finished reading about Shauna's cooking club, I shut the book and contacted the five women I most wanted to glean from. Our village was formed.

Of the six of us, five have adopted children and two have kids with Down syndrome. Together, we have a total of twenty-seven kids, fifteen of whom are adopted, and counting! Yes, we are, in fact, a small village.

We all come from different walks of life and have different ways of raising our kids. That day, I needed their listening ears and honest, transparent input. I told them about what had happened with Truly at my parents' house. This was not the first time they had heard this sort of account from me. They were familiar with the challenges I was facing as Truly's mom. As I buried my head in my hands, again, and cried tears of frustration, again, my friend Cynthia interrupted me.

"Heather, this is totally normal. You know that, right?" Cynthia is mother to eight kids, three of whom are adopted. "I have less than lovely feelings toward one of my natural-born kids. And yeah, it sucks."

"Me too," my friend Laura chimed in. "You *know* who my difficult child is. The way you describe your feelings toward Truly is often how I feel toward the child I gave birth to."

As we continued to talk, I realized we all have a child who is more difficult than our other ones, a child who squashes our warm-fuzzy feelings. For some, these negative feelings stem from a lack of bonding and the trauma their adopted kids faced before being placed in their adoptive home. For others in our group, adoption has nothing to do with it. They simply have a child who is more difficult to like.

I loved these women for being so real. I can't adequately describe the sense of peace I get when something in my life is normalized. Not feeling warm and fuzzy toward our children isn't something most moms ever talk about. So many of us have a child who is challenging to enjoy. Friends, I want to tell you that it's okay.

What happened that day over coffee with my friends opened a

door for me to release the guilt I was feeling and begin to explore my love for Truly in a new way. I realized that my emotions did not determine my love for her.

The apostle Paul writes the following about love:

> Love is patient, love is kind. It does not envy, it does not boast, it is not proud. It does not dishonor others, it is not self-seeking, it is not easily angered, it keeps no record of wrongs. Love does not delight in evil but rejoices with the truth. It always protects, always trusts, always hopes, always perseveres.
>
> *1 Corinthians 13:4–7*

Love is not an emotion. Love is not a feeling. Love is 100 percent an action. As a person who grew up reading this Bible passage, I knew this. But God, in his good, good grace, was teaching me *his* love in new ways. I had come so far in giving up control and allowing God's best for my life to unfold around me, but I had failed to see the envy, pride, and selfishness hiding in my heart. Ouch!

Yes, Truly was a challenge, but the real issue was me. I needed to continue to be refined. I needed to continue to learn what real, true, and meaningful love is.

As the months and years have gone on, I've discovered my lack of emotional warm fuzzies toward Truly have in fact created a stronger, more meaningful love for her. I love her! I love her so much. I wake up every day and am able to show her patience, kindness, and honor. I make an extra effort to put her needs before my own. I do everything in my power to protect her. And by loving her this way with the love of Jesus, my hope is that the full weight of my love will root itself deep into her soul. I hope that when she thinks of love, she doesn't think of warm-fuzzy emotions but of how I love her in action.

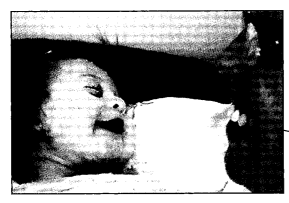

Our first visit with Macyn at her foster home.

Heather loving on Macyn during a visit at her foster home.

Josh's mom meets Macyn for the first time.

The people-less baby shower our friends surprised us with.

Macyn the day after her surgery.

Heather's sister and parents meet Macyn for the first time.

Josh holds Macyn for the first time after her surgery.

Macyn with her biological grandfather and sister the day we met in the park.

Macyn on a walk the day after we got to take her off oxygen.

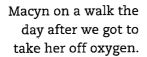

Macyn at Christmas 2011.

Family photo when Macyn was two.

The day we met Truly at her foster home—she would come home with us a few days later.

Macyn is so excited to be a big sister.

The day we brought Truly home—she fell asleep in the car!

Our first day as a family of four.

Heather, Macyn, and Truly with Harmony, Hana, and Heather's mom on the day Truly came home.

The first time we held August on the day he was born.

Birth mom and me the day August was born.

Loving their new brother, Christmas 2013.

Family photo—our new family of five.

August's birth mom holds him while his heart surgeon does one last check before taking him back for open-heart surgery.

August gives his mommy a smile two days after his open-heart surgery.

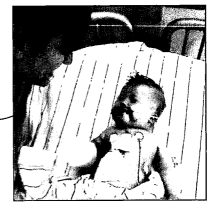

August and his dad!

Hanging out in Augie's crib.

The *Lucky Few* crew.

Karen Marie Photography (karenmarieco.com)

My sweet daughters
and me, 2016.

I'm the luckiest girl I know
(Macyn, 8; Truly, 5; August, 2).

Michelle Sullivan Photography (michellesullivanphotography.com)

The Avis family.

Michelle Sullivan Photography (michellesullivanphotography.com)

I still have days when I want to lock Truly in her room and turn up the music to drown out her dramatic sobs. I still have days when I am convinced I'm ruining her, squelching her feisty little spirit because it makes me have to work harder as a mom. But more than that, I have great hope, knowing that God loves Truly too. I believe he is molding and shaping her curiosity, strong will, determined spirit, and ability to connect emotionally. Just like he's doing for me, he is refining Truly for his purposes and his glory. I'm learning that these struggles and feelings I have do not determine the kind of mom I am or the love I have for my Truly Star.

In fact, I often feel as though I am to God what Truly is to me. I wake up every day fighting to be the one in control, believing I know what is best, pushing the boundaries that God has lovingly placed around me. Yet in his vast love for me, God gave me my Truly Star so I could learn how to love. How to really, really love so I could experience *his* love—his true love for me.

10

God's Got This

Two kids are a lot of kids. I'm sure some of you who have more than two kids are smiling and thinking, *Well, bless your heart for thinking so*. No matter, I still believe that two kids are a lot of kids. And I was convinced that my two kids were a bigger handful than most. Combining Macyn's numerous weekly occupational, physical, and speech therapies and medical appointments with Truly's zeal for life, I found my plate overflowing.

I wanted to be the person who saw an overflowing plate as a beautiful gift. I wanted to be the mom who fully embraced each season of my children's growth and could spot the joy and beauty amid the chaos. But when my friends would say things like, "I just want to embrace this season," I'd be thinking, *I want out!*

When Macyn and Truly were around ages four and two, I felt as though I was at my actual maximum capacity. My plate was so full that I believed if a third child were to enter my life at that moment, my physical body would break, perhaps split in two right down the middle.

During this particular time, several friends were on their own adoption journeys, and they would call me at random hours to announce, "Guess what? We're getting a baby!" Every time, along with great jubilation, I would feel a tiny twitch of jealousy.

I would hang up the phone, find Josh, and announce, "I want a baby."

He would lovingly remind me of our reality. Then mealtime or bedtime would roll around, and within an hour, I would turn to my husband and say, "Never mind my crazy talk. We're good. No need for a baby right here, right now."

Still, the pattern showed me that my heart longed for a third Avis kid. When the timing was right.

Having two adoptions under our belt, Josh and I knew that if we wanted to grow our family via an adoption again (which was still our only option), it made sense to start the process during this crazy, full season of parenthood, knowing it would likely take at least a year for a child to be placed in our home. By then, I would be "ready" (whatever that means) to have a third child.

Toward the end of September 2013, we made an appointment to attend our county's monthly "taking care of business" day. It was the same event we had attended when we began our process to adopt Truly Star. Because this was our second county adoption, we learned we would be fast-tracked through the line. So we took our daughters with us.

Afterward we posed as a family outside of the building and asked someone to snap our picture while we held up the application for the newest Avis child. Then we plastered that photo all over our social media. It was our way of announcing our kind of "pregnancy." Right away, friends posted kind words and wished us well on the journey. It felt good to take this first step, trusting we would need to take at least a year's worth of steps before we welcomed our new munchkin.

Famous last words.

I feel an instant affinity with everyone I meet who has a child with Down syndrome, or who has adopted, or who has adopted a child with Down syndrome. We share an unspoken understanding, as if we're members of the coolest of clubs—the kind of club located in the scary-looking building downtown with the entrance hidden behind the old, creeping vines. But once you find the courage to step inside, you realize it's the most beautiful and exciting place you've ever laid eyes on, and you feel gosh darn lucky to be there.

In early October, I received a phone call from one of these club members, my dear friend Mercedes. This woman may be one of the most joy-filled humans I've ever known. She's the kind of person you can't help but adore and love to be around. She's funny and kind and genuine and looks at life through the most optimistic of lenses. She and her husband had recently adopted a little girl with Down syndrome.

"Hey, Merc. Love hearing from you. What's going on?"

"Well . . ." Her voice teetered between anxious and elated. She went with elated. "I just had a woman contact me who's looking for a family to adopt her son who has Down syndrome." She offered the news to me like a new car or an all-expenses-paid trip to Disney World.

I received this news like a kick in the gut. My silence left her with room to continue.

"Okay, here's the scoop: This mom contacted me because the site we had our adoption profile on never took it down. She wanted to know if we want to adopt her baby, but I told her we just brought Sunflower home, so we can't. Then I remembered seeing the picture you and Josh posted on Facebook. Since you guys are starting the adopting process again, of course I thought of you."

The air that had been knocked out of me found its way back into my lungs.

"Whoa. This is crazy, Mercedes. Ahhh! What in the world? Tell me what you know."

"Okay, well, she's seven months pregnant, and the baby is due in December. It's a *boy*." She said *boy* slowly, with a hint of contagious joy in her voice. "He does have a heart defect, but I think that's all. Mom's name is Sami." She paused and then added, "And I think you should adopt this baby."

"Mercedes, we're not ready for a third baby. I need another year, not two months! Girl, why'd you have to go and tell me about this baby?"

"But, Heather, a boy! With Down syndrome!" She laughed a contagious laugh. "This is not the kind of thing we pass up."

I knew she was right. I knew as soon as I heard the words "this mom . . ." Yet this was so outside of my plans and, more importantly, outside of my capacity. A third child was one thing, but a third child who has Down syndrome and will need lifesaving open-heart surgery—in *this* current season of life?

"Girl, I am so mad at you for opening this door for me." My tone was playful, but I felt my body begin to rip at the seams. The truth was that I really did feel a little bit angry at this situation.

I wasn't angry at Mercedes for calling my attention to this mom and her unborn son. I was angry that once Mercedes spoke the words, I could no longer go on with life as it was. God knew how full my plate was, and he knew he had created my heart to long for these kinds of opportunities, yet he allowed these words to find their way to my ears.

Really, God? I thought to myself. *You knew when I found out about this baby I would have to start taking steps toward him. Why do you do this all the time?*

Mercedes interrupted my silent rant.

"At least have a conversation with her. I told her all about you and Josh, and she really wants to talk. Hey, I'll give her your Facebook information, and you can talk through Messenger. See, it's not even that serious if you're talking through Messenger." She laughed.

"Okay. I guess. I'll talk to her. But gosh, girl, why do you have to go and stir things up in the Avis home? My cup is full . . . *to the brim.*"

Mercedes laughed. "You've got this. A baby. A boy. With Down syndrome. You know you can't say no."

She was right. As I hung up the phone, my heart settled somewhere between utter terror and complete joy.

I turned on an episode of *Signing Time!* for my girls so I could open my laptop with minimal interruptions. As soon as I opened Facebook, I saw a friend request atop the tiny icon. I clicked on it, and the request was from a woman named Sami—and Mercedes was our only mutual friend. There was also a message from her in my Messenger app. With butterflies in my stomach, I opened the message.

Hi, Heather,

I was given your name by Mercedes. She mentioned you're starting the adoption process for your third child. I am currently seven months pregnant and will send you the info I had given Mercedes as a starting point.

We found out at twenty-six weeks that we are having a boy. We also found out at that visit that he has a hole in his heart, a complete atrioventricular canal defect. Wow! What overwhelming news that was. We were immediately taken to meet with a genetic counselor, and additional appointments were set up for a fetal echo, etc. We were past the point where they could safely do an amnio, so I had a blood test done to determine what we were facing. The doctors told us this defect is usually associated with Down syndrome. Our results came back Monday positive for Down syndrome.

We have decided that adoption for our sweet boy is the most loving thing we can do for him. It is the hardest thing I have EVER faced in all my life. I know God has a plan. I know at this point I don't understand so many things, but I have faith and know all will work out according to his will. The most

important thing to me is finding a loving home for our sweet
boy that can provide what we feel we are not able to.

Please let me know if you're interested in learning more
or if you have any questions.

I read and reread Sami's message. I thought about how this day
was supposed to be a normal day full of making meals, building towers,
and painting tiny fingernails. Today was not supposed to be one for the
books. I couldn't believe this was happening. I copied and pasted the
note into a message for Josh and included a sassy message of my own.

What the heck? The timing sucks. You know we can't say no.
Can we say no? Ahhhhhhh!

While I waited for his reply, I accepted Sami's friend request and
began looking at every photo she had in her account. I saw pictures
of her son and daughter. Photos of her with people I assumed were
her mom and dad and sisters. Then I saw a recent photo of her with a
swollen belly. She wore a bright orange dress and stood beside a tall,
handsome man who had his arm around her. I thought this might be
the birth father, and the baby in her belly—the son I might one day
call my own. Gulp!

A reply from Josh popped up on my screen.

This is crazy! I think we need to adopt him.

With his simple reply, Josh confirmed what I knew in my gut.

I couldn't believe this was happening. I could never go back to
the person I was before finding out about this baby, but not because
I thought I was his only answer. God had been showing me over the

years that I'm not here to be a rescuer. My job is to lift up my foot and trust God, *my* rescuer, to set it down exactly where he sees fit, whether it's in the mud or on a ledge. As soon as I answered the phone call from Mercedes, I knew this was God placing my foot down . . . on a ledge!

Still, I didn't want to fully believe it. Not right away. I sat on the floor of my living room staring at the words on my computer screen, feeling so conflicted. On the one hand, there was this baby boy who happened to have Down syndrome, and with one yes, he could be mine forever. On the other hand, there was this baby boy who happened to have Down syndrome, and with one no, I could go on with life and wait for the next baby to come by. I could wait until I was ready. I could wait for a baby who was healthy.

No seemed like the smart answer. Like the answer any reasonable person would give. I mean, who in the world adopts two children with Down syndrome? Who in the world signs up, *again*, for a baby who will need open-heart surgery? As I asked myself these questions, I looked at my Macyn Hope and my Truly Star sitting on the couch singing and signing along with Rachel, Alex, Leah, and Hopkins. I looked at those girls and thought of the yes they each represented. I thought of how God, by his good, good grace, put the yes in my mouth. I thought about what my life might have looked like if I had thought rationally all those years ago and said no to adopting Macyn or no to adopting Truly, and I began to cry. What kind of person says yes to adopting a little boy with Down syndrome and a heart defect?

"Me! I do!" I said out loud. I closed my computer and sat on the couch between my girls.

"I love you so much, girls," I said through the tears.

"You have tears, Mommy?" Truly asked as she turned to look at me with her big, brown, sparkly eyes.

"I do, baby, but they're good tears. They are happy tears, because

I love you and your sister so, so, so, so much, and I'm so happy I get to be your mommy."

Truly looked at my face for a little bit longer, and then, apparently satisfied, she turned back to the TV. I pulled her onto my lap, and together we sang and signed the words "sun, sun, sun, sunny day."

Josh and I said yes to adopting this baby boy, and things began to move quickly. We signed up with an adoption agency, and they fast-tracked us through background checks, piles and piles of paperwork, and a home study. Facebook friend requests and messages from Sami's two sisters and her mom started rolling in. As they gently asked us about our family and hinted at wanting to remain a part of their nephew's and grandson's life, we discovered how supported and loved both Sami and our son were.

It was awkward at first. Even though our relationship with Macyn's birth family had changed our opinions about the matter, we had never been so quickly and closely connected to a birth family. Social media platforms opened a door for an instant, intimate look into each other's lives. There were so many people involved, which means so many different feelings and opinions and expectations. Never before did I need to let go of control like I did with this adoption. When conversations with the birth family became especially intimate, I would find myself trying to direct the situation at hand. Then I would feel the Lord nudge me and remind me to pursue this child with hands wide open, hopeful and eager to see God be glorified in every step.

It was a difficult way for this recovering control freak to bring this baby into her fold! The whole situation began to overwhelm me, and I began to second-guess every part.

One morning in late October, I received a text from Sami inviting me to an echocardiogram. I was thrilled because I had never been able to know my children while they were being knit together in their mother's womb. To see my baby and hear his heartbeat on an ultrasound machine was a small dream I had let go of years ago. This invitation was an answer to my heart's desire.

In order to hear this heartbeat, I would be meeting Sami for the first time. The woman growing my son in her body. The woman whose facial features my son will have, whose DNA my son will share. The woman whose sacrifice will result in my great joy.

Adoptive parents have to embrace the intermingling of tragedy and joy. For me, the complexity is a constant reminder of a Savior who had to die so we might experience life. So many times, I've wished I could just sit in the joy of it all! Then I would remember that I can only fully know the joy when I accept the heartbreak as well.

Sami's in utero echocardiogram was scheduled to take place on a Friday afternoon. I had plans to attend a women's retreat that weekend with two of my best friends and their church. Early that day, I got my girls settled with the grandparents. I'd already prepped and frozen meals for my husband. I grabbed my weekend getaway bag and a bag of small gifts and gift cards for Sami, and I got in the car and started my two-hour drive to the San Diego hospital where the echocardiogram would take place. The hospital my son would be born in.

I arrived a few minutes early and made my way to the fountain at the front entrance where Sami and I had agreed to meet. A coastal fog hung thick in the air. It was a typical Southern California winter day. I paced around the fountain, trying to spot the face of the woman in the photos, searching for a swollen belly. I watched as parents and children came and went. I had spent many hours as a face and a story at another children's hospital with Macyn. I looked at faces and wondered what their stories were—why they were here. I thought about why I was here. As I battled the overwhelming nerves taking over my body, I thought about how this was not the story I had written for myself. I thought about how the last thing I wanted to do right then was sit for hours with the stranger who would give me her baby. Once again, I began to second-guess the arrangement.

As I paced the fountain and watched water splash onto the ground, I felt the Lord say to me, "Don't forget who I am. I've got this. This is what I do. Now you do what I've designed you to do."

I was flooded by memories of Macyn as a tiny infant, sick, at death's door. And of Truly as a feisty baby, pushing me to the edge of myself. And there, in the midst of it all: God. God and his goodness and faithfulness enveloping me. God, being all I need and showing up every single time. If things were comfortable and easy—if I did not have adoption and Down syndrome and heart defects and birth parents and babies with someone else's eyes, hair, and skin tone—I would not have needed God as desperately as I had. And if I had not needed him, or rather, if I had not recognized my need for him, I would not have known him.

"Sweet daughter," I heard him whisper as I waited for Sami to show up, "here I am, in the discomfort. Find comfort in me. I've got this."

I closed my eyes and breathed him in, thinking to myself, *He's got this.* When I opened my eyes, I saw Sami heading my way. Our eyes met, and we smiled at one another. I gave a little wave, and as I walked toward her, I prayed I wouldn't puke.

"Hey, Sami, I'm Heather." I wrapped my arms around her neck, unable to ignore her belly pushing against mine. My initial embrace with Sami, and my first contact with my son. This was really happening.

"I'm so nervous," Sami blurted out.

Her honesty calmed my nerves a bit. "Me too!" I shared.

We stood there awkwardly for what felt like an eternity.

"We should go inside," she said. "It's a bit of a trek to the section of the hospital where the echos are done."

I followed Sami through the automatic sliding doors. As we zigzagged through hallways, climbed stairs, and rode elevators, the moments of silence were plentiful.

Sami was tall, like me. She had blonde hair and striking blue eyes. She was slender, except for her bulging belly. And she was an introvert.

As we made our way through the hospital and to the waiting area, I reminded myself that her quiet and shy demeanor was not a reflection of her bravery. The extrovert in me had at least one million things to talk about. I wanted to know how she was feeling and every detail of the pregnancy so far. I wanted to know the ins and outs of her decision-making process. I wanted her to pour out her heart to me and for us to hold one another and cry and become lifelong friends. I wanted to touch her belly and feel the baby move. But I followed her lead and kept it all to myself.

We arrived at the waiting area, a small square room with rows of colorful chairs. I sat down as Sami checked in. She joined me and began to fill out forms on a clipboard. We sat there in a deafening quiet.

"So you have two older kids?" I asked questions I already knew the answers to as a way to break the silence trying to suffocate me.

"Yes."

"How old are they?"

"Eight and twelve."

Awkward silence. I just couldn't stand it.

"And what about this baby's birth father? Are you comfortable with telling me more about him?"

She shrugged. "We've been dating for a while. But when he found out the baby has a heart defect, it was too much for him. He decided he wasn't going to parent even before the Down syndrome diagnosis." The quiver in her voice and pain in her eyes told me not to push more on the subject.

"I'm so sorry to hear that, Sami. So, how have you been feeling? I mean physically?"

"I'm feeling okay."

Silence. I gave up. I thought about my desire for her to open up to me and remembered that we were not there as friends. We sat together as something so much more. Mothers. Mothers who love the same baby. Mothers willing to sacrifice everything for an unborn child. Mothers with very different roles.

I sat in that waiting room with my hands folded tightly on my lap because I did not trust them to stay away from Sami's belly. Yet I knew I needed to keep my hands to myself. I needed to respect her role as this baby's mother right now. I needed to wait my turn, for it would last a lifetime. She would have the sole title of mother for these short nine months. This day, the day when I would get to hear my unborn baby's heartbeat, was not about me at all. So while we waited and I held my hands on my lap, I opened my clenched fists as a way of remembering to let go of my need to control this situation.

A technician came in. "Sami?"

We both stood up and followed him to a dimly lit room. In the middle of the room was an exam table lined with white paper. Next to it was the same kind of machine used to show us pictures of Macyn's heart. Next to the big machine were two small black chairs. I set my purse on one and sat in the other, as close as I could get to the screen that would be displaying the images of my son's broken heart.

Sami excused herself to use the restroom. As I settled in, the technician asked, "So are you family or a friend?"

This one innocent question was almost too complicated to answer.

I never thought to ask Sami if this adoption was public knowledge. I sat there looking at the technician, unsure if it was my place to answer such an innocent question.

We looked at each other for a few awkward moments before I answered, "Both I guess. I actually just met Sami today because I'm going to be adopting her baby."

The technician's stunned silence was enough to communicate how out of left field my answer was. As we continued with the day's theme of awkward silence, Sami came back in the room, and I blurted out, "I told him I'm adopting your baby. I hope that's okay."

She gave a small smile. "Oh, of course." Then she lay on the paper-lined bed and lifted her sweater to reveal her belly.

Hearing and seeing my son's heartbeat was a beautiful experience. For more than an hour, I sat and watched this tiny heart beating while the technician took hundreds of pictures for the cardiologist. When he had gathered all the images he needed, we waited, in silence, for the cardiologist to come in and go over the findings with us.

There was a light knock on the door, and he walked in, head down, studying the results of the echo.

"Sami. It is good to see you again." He looked up. "How are you feeling?"

"I'm feeling okay."

"The results are the same, which is to be expected." He glanced at me and then back at Sami. "But it does not mean the baby has Down syndrome."

"He does," she answered plainly. "I had the blood test done, and it came back positive."

"Oh, I see." The cardiologist looked back and forth between us.

I simply smiled at him, silently praying that Sami would take the reins and introduce me.

"I'm choosing an adoption plan." Sami motioned toward me. "This is Heather. She's going to be adopting the baby."

"Hi." I gave a little wave.

"Oh, hi. It's nice to meet you. Do you have any questions for me?"

"Yes." I pulled out a notebook I'd become accustomed to bringing with me to appointments. "I have quite a few, if that's okay."

"Of course." The cardiologist sat in the chair next to mine.

I opened the notebook and began to go through my dozen or so questions. The cardiologist answered each one in frank detail as I diligently took notes. I got to the end of my list knowing one fact clearly: this baby had a serious heart defect that would require open-heart surgery at least.

I closed my notebook, and we all sat there for a minute in the heaviness of the situation. Then the cardiologist looked at Sami and with grand hope declared, "I do believe you could not have found a more wonderful mother for your son."

Sami and I looked at one another and smiled.

The words offered so much more than I'm sure he intended. As we walked this adoption path together, both Sami and I knew that every word of affirmation along the way was pure gold.

I tucked my notebook into my purse, gave Sami a big squeeze, and left the hospital. As my wheels hit the freeway, I had an overwhelming urge to throw up. Meeting Sami and talking to the doctor left me with a heavy load of fear and anxiety. I spent the next couple of hours in the car, trying to wrap my head around it all.

I felt like a crazy person. Crazy for feeling so much fear and anxiety. Crazy for saying yes to this adoption. Crazy for feeling so nauseated all the time. It was as if with each adoption, I was having my own unique kind of morning sickness! I was overwhelmed with the need to make it all go away. I wanted to call Sami and tell her it was too much for me. I wanted to wake up tomorrow with my two beautiful daughters and make breakfast, and do dishes and sit comfortably in the world I knew so well.

I sat in traffic on my way to see my friends for the women's retreat sobbing and trying to catch my breath. There I was again, flailing around and trying to grab hold of something—anything that would tell me for sure that this baby would be okay. While I groped around for some kind of control, God slapped me in the face with a flood of memories about Macyn.

I started thinking back to when we said yes to adopting Macyn. I remembered that it was this same month, five years ago. I remembered having a similar conversation with a cardiologist. I remembered feeling as though I was going to puke all the time from nerves and anxiety. As I sobbed in my car, I remembered clearly what it was like to walk in faith during that season. I remembered knowing God in a way I never had before. I remembered his favor being poured out on me in ways I could never have imagined. I remembered the joy and peace he lavished on me as I stepped into her adoption. And when I looked back, searching for it, I couldn't even find a glimpse of tragedy, because it had been covered and enveloped by beauty.

Then I heard God say again to me, "Don't forget who I am. I've got this. This is what I do. Now you do what I've designed you to do."

Two hours later, I pulled up to the hotel where the women's retreat was being held. I drove past the entrance and saw my friends Erika and Laura waiting for me by the automatic door. I got out of the car and stepped into the chilly night air, pulling my coat tighter around my body.

Laura and Erika are two of the women in my village. I had known them during the months leading up to our bringing Macyn home. They sat with me in hospital rooms, praying over my fragile daughter and bringing me coffee and no-bake cookies to help keep me awake through the nights. They showed up at my house on December 15, 2008, the day we took Macyn off her oxygen, and jumped and screamed and shouted and praised God with us over the work of his hands and the healing of our daughter. They were the first friends to get a text message with that first photo of our Truly Star, and once she came home, they were the people who brought me trays of homemade lasagna and big pots of creamy soup.

As soon as I learned about the life growing in Sami's womb, they were among the first ones I called to share the news of the opportunity at hand. They had been with me, both spiritually and literally, every step of the way.

My friends had big, goofy smiles on their faces, excited to hear about how the appointment went.

"Soooo?" they asked simultaneously, as though they had practiced. Their eyes were full of buckets of hope. As soon as our eyes met, buckets of tears began to fill mine. I fell into their arms and sobbed.

"Oh no." Laura looked at Erika. "What happened?"

"Nothing happened. I mean everything happened." I stood up straight. "I don't know!" I put my head in my hands and continued to sob.

Erika and Laura put their arms around me.

"This is too hard," I managed to say as I gulped air between sobs. "I wish it would all just go away."

"Did something go wrong? Is the baby okay?" Erika inquired.

"It was fine. Sami was sweet and generous. The baby's heart is not good, but it's exactly what I expected. But I think I'm crazy for doing this. Who does this? Am I crazy?" I looked at Erika with pleading eyes, praying she held the answers I sought. Erika and her husband had four adopted children under the age of five. I had been with them for each and every one.

"Of course you're crazy." Erika smiled at me. "But it's the *best* kind of crazy!" Laura nodded in agreement.

"Why do I feel like this? Why am I more terrified about bringing this baby home than I am excited?" I sniffed. "Does that mean I should say no?"

"Well, I don't think you should say no just because you feel scared," Erika said.

"I agree," Laura chimed in. "Heather, adopting another child with Down syndrome *is* a big deal, and adopting a child with a heart defect *is* a big deal. I think feeling terrified *is* a normal feeling."

"Really?" That word *normal* brought me so much peace. I let the encouragement from my friends sink in.

"So you don't think I should say no?" I asked again, half hoping they'd tell me I should, half hoping they'd tell me I shouldn't.

"No!" they said at the exact same time. They put their arms around me again. "You should adopt this baby."

I took a deep breath. "Okay then." And the three of us walked through the sliding doors and joined the rest of the women.

I'm so thankful for the timing of the retreat. I believe it was not a coincidence that I got to spend three days away from my hectic life at home in the midst of a difficult decision. These days were full of prayer and reflection and lots of life-giving conversations with women I love and respect. It was exactly what I needed, at exactly the right time.

When I got home from the retreat, Josh and I set aside some rare alone time to talk about the heavy doubts I had after meeting Sami and talking with the cardiologist. He already knew how terrified I felt.

"If you think so strongly that we're supposed to adopt this baby, why am I so doubtful?" I sat on one end of our white couch and tucked my legs up under me.

"We've been parents of a child with Down syndrome for five years. We've walked in the valley of the shadow of death as our sweet baby girl underwent a lifesaving open-heart surgery. We came out on the other side, with Macyn alive and well. We've watched and cheered as our almost three-year-old took her first step. We've spent the past five years knowing that what God has given us in Macyn is nothing less than a gift, and only the lucky few receive it." I nodded, tears in my eyes, as Josh continued. "I believe that for this baby. You can't let your feelings get in the way of the truth of God's goodness."

This was exactly what I needed to hear. I kept nodding, speechless. Josh scooted closer to me and wrapped his arms around me.

"God's got this, babe."

"God's got this."

My time at the retreat and my conversation with Josh were pivotal in how I continued to take steps toward our son's adoption. Neither occurrence erased all of the fears I had, mostly fears of the unknown attached to this baby, but both became strong pillars of sorts. Assurance I could lean on when my knees went weak.

Honestly, during those two months, I felt doubtful more often than I felt confident. I seemed to have some sort of amnesia triggered by the potential difficulties of the whole situation. Day after day, I kept forgetting all that God had done. I had trouble remembering his calling over my life. Yet by his good, good, good grace, he continued to whisper into the dark corners of my heart: "Don't forget who I am. I've got this. This is what I do. Now you do what I've designed you to do."

11

Joy and Heartbreak

"Wake up." Josh was gently pushing on my shoulder. "Babe, you need to wake up."

"What time is it?" I asked as I slowly opened my eyes and rolled over to look at Josh, who was sitting on the edge of the bed.

"It's seven," he said with a big, goofy grin. "He was born. August was born."

I jolted up in bed. "Are you kidding? You're kidding. Tell me the truth."

"Heather, I wouldn't joke about this." Josh laughed. "August was born at two thirty this morning. No induction needed. There were a bunch of texts and missed calls on your phone."

"My phone was on silent?" I grabbed it out of Josh's hands. "Is he okay? We need to go. I need him. Is he okay?"

"He's fine." Josh gave me a reassuring squeeze. "He's perfect."

"What did she say?" I began to read the text messages from Sami's sister Lucy, announcing my son's entrance into the world.

"He's here!" I shouted.

"He's here!" Josh echoed.

I am a bit of a birth junkie. I love all things birth. I attribute this to being raised by a mother who went drug-free through three labors that each lasted more than twenty-four hours. She believes words such as *epidural* and *Pitocin* are worse than the F-word. My parents were Bradley Method birth instructors, and my childhood is sprinkled with memories of our living room full of dads holding on to their wives' bulging bellies. The "hee whooo" of their breathing exercises often lulled me to sleep. And if you've been to my childhood home more than a few times, then my mom has asked you if you'd like to see Hana's birth video.

I will never forget feeding my sister Harmony ice chips, holding her leg and weeping as she suffered the inevitable pain of childbirth. Then I shed tears of celebration as my nephew, and later my niece, took first breaths and uttered first cries. There is simply nothing like it in the world.

Truth be told, if you are pregnant or hoping to become pregnant, I'll try to chat with you about your ovulation cycle, your birth plan, the baby's name, and whether there is room for me in the hospital room. (I'm an excellent leg holder and ice-chip feeder.) I may ask all of this before I even know your name. I also recognize that my hope to one day deliver a baby on a plane, on a train, or on the middle of a busy sidewalk is, in fact, something every pregnant woman would like to avoid.

There is just something spectacular about a human growing another human.

Toward the beginning of my journey as a mother, my love of this creation miracle only increased the pain of my infertility. It was fuel on my fire. But the thing about fire is that it has the power and ability to burn away impurities, leaving us more refined. For me, this purification began with mourning the loss of my body's ability to create new life. I also had to release an unhealthy jealousy of those who get to partake in the miracle. As the refining process burned up that jealousy, I found myself walking out of the fire with utter gratefulness for my perky boobs and stretch-mark-free midsection. Now that I find myself on the other side of the fire, my prayer involves a slight plea that I will *never* experience pregnancy. If Josh and I choose to continue to grow our family, my hope is that it will only be through adoption. *Please, dear Jesus, not in my body.* This is not vanity talking, but gratefulness—and an awareness that God has completely healed me. My desire to have a baby naturally holds no power over me any longer.

Still, even refined, I will always wish I could have been present on the days my girls were born. Adoption creates longing within every person involved. For me, the longing to be my children's mother from their first breath, to be the one whose heartbeat offered instant comfort in the strange world outside of the womb, will forever go unfilled. Yet when I held my girls at night as they peacefully slept in my arms, by God's grace this action alone would melt away my sorrow over all that I had missed.

When Sami entered my life and I learned she was still pregnant, I thought, *This is my chance,* and I prayed she would invite me to be at the birth. I wanted to catch the baby and hold his slippery, swollen, perfect little body in my arms. Maybe, when his eyes opened that first time for one brief second to take in the new world around him, I would be the first blurry face he would see.

But she didn't invite me, and I never asked. We were strangers after all, and her support system was mighty. She did not need me to be my son's first mother. I imagine she needed that for herself. I imagine she needed him to know that her love for him was fierce and endless. He could soak it in as he sat, slippery and swollen, on her chest, listening to the heartbeat of that love. I imagine she prayed that the love she could offer him during those first moments of his life would seep deep into his veins, saturating every cell in his body so she would forever be a part of him.

I read and reread the text from Sami's sister. I quickly texted Lucy, letting her know my phone had been in silent mode. I asked her what Sami wanted us to do. As I waited for her reply, I grabbed a suitcase and starting throwing clothes into it. I hoped to get in the car as soon as possible and head to the hospital, which was two hours away.

My phone dinged.

> **Lucy:** I'm not sure what Sami wants just yet. She hasn't really said. But he's perfect, Heather. Do you want me to send a picture of him, or do you want to wait and see him yourself?

> **Me:** A picture please! I don't think I can wait any longer.

Then my phone gave another ding, and there he was, August Ryker, my majestic and vulnerable son. I gasped at his perfection. He was more adorable than I could have dreamed up. He had a head full of hair, and it was spiked into a perfect little mohawk. His almond-shaped eyes, turned-down mouth, and button nose were those of a child with Down syndrome, no doubt. He was wrapped in a muslin blanket the color of the sea and sky. I later found out Sami had lovingly made it for him. I held my phone, staring at this perfect human, God's intention, and laughed and cried and shouted right there in my bedroom, "Thank you, Jesus, for the gift of this child. Thank you, Jesus, for my son."

We finally got the thumbs-up from Lucy to head to the hospital. We dropped off the girls at my dad's office, the same office where we had prayed about adopting Macyn. My dad, "the crier" as he's known, could hardly speak, he was so choked up. We pulled out of the parking lot waving to Macyn and Truly, who were each holding one of his hands.

We arrived in the late afternoon, and my arms were beginning to feel the void. I texted Lucy to let her know we were there. She told us to make our way to the sixth floor and gave us the room number.

It was a beautiful Southern California December day. The sun was shining with just the right amount of chill in the air. Josh and I parked our car on the third level of the hospital's parking garage and made our way hand in hand down the steps. We approached the sliding glass doors of the entrance, and they opened as though to usher us into a magical land. I squeezed Josh's hand, and we walked in.

We found Sami's room and gently knocked on the door. The door opened, and Josh and I were greeted by a warm smile and kind blue eyes. "Hi, I'm Tandy, Sami's mom. So good to finally meet you both." Tandy was as tall as I am, with blonde hair and a warmth that instantly eased the tension that might have been present in such a situation.

"Congratulations, Grandma," Josh replied as he wrapped his arms around her and gave her a big hug.

I too found myself in her embrace. Then she said, "Come in and meet your son."

We walked around the privacy curtain hanging from the ceiling. My eyes scanned the room and fell on the tiny, perfect human wrapped in his blue muslin blanket, cradled in Sami's arms. I wanted to hurry over to him, scoop him up, and kiss him a thousand times. I wanted him on my chest, hearing and feeling the heartbeat of my love. I wanted to spend the next hours, days, lifetime, looking at his face and whispering in his ear, "Hey, sweet guy, it's your mama. I love you so."

But this was not our room, and on this day, I was not his only mama. We walked through the doors as guests in our own story. So I controlled my urge to grab him, and instead I made my way to the hospital bed and wrapped my arms tightly around Sami.

"I was doing so well, but now I'm going to cry," she said as we held on to each other. Both of us shed tears.

"You doing okay?" I asked her as we loosened our embrace and I sat back a bit to look her in the eyes. She nodded and then looked down at the baby in her arms. I followed her gaze and exhaled a bit. "Oh Sami, he's beyond perfect. I can't believe he's here."

"Wanna hold him?" she asked.

"Yes!" I nearly shouted. "Let me wash my hands." I stood to walk to the bathroom, which was no more than three feet from the foot of Sami's bed. The whole room was a small square, no more than ten feet by ten feet. The bed took up most of the room. To the right of her bed was a bassinet for August. A large window overlooked the freeway, and under the window was a padded bench that could be folded down into a small bed. Sitting on the bench were Sami's two sisters and her daughter.

Josh had been chatting with the sisters, Lucy and Brittany, while Sami and I cried in each other's arms. Before I made my way to the bathroom, I stopped to give each of them a hug. They shared their mother's blonde hair and kind blue eyes.

"It's so nice to finally meet you both," I said. Then I sat on the bench next to Sami's daughter, Joy, and put my arm around her. "Congratulations, big sister. What do you think of your baby brother?"

"He's cute," she sweetly replied.

As Josh and I washed our hands, Tandy pulled up two chairs near the foot of the bed, and when I walked out of the bathroom, she handed me my son. As soon as I felt his tiny body in my arms, my whole being flooded with adoration and love. My son! He was the definition of perfection. I'm sure every mother has ideas and visions of what their unborn child will look like. As soon as I laid eyes on him, I knew no image had ever entered my mind that was as beautiful as the baby in my arms was.

As I stared at the features on his perfectly formed face, I thought about the previous weeks and how terrified I was of the idea of him. As I held him close and felt his heartbeat next to mine, every fear I had seemed to melt away. I knew the tiny heart was sick and fragile, and the baby in my arms had an extra chromosome, but I could not remember what I had been so afraid of. The baby in my arms was a dreamboat. As I inhaled the scent of him, I could hardly believe my luck.

Josh and I knew our place that day in that room. The situation at hand was unique, and the complex emotions that were present touched each of us in different and at times confusing ways. There, in this tiny hospital room, resided two adoring aunties, a grinning grandma, a proud big sister, a brave and selfless birth mom, excited adoptive parents, and the one who brought us together—this perfect little boy, August Ryker.

We spent the rest of that evening taking turns holding him. Commenting on his amazing hair and perfect complexion. *Oohing* and *aahing* over every lovely finger and wrinkle. We talked and told stories and got to know one another. We tiptoed around a bit, knowing how delicate the situation was, how many full hearts were involved. We respected each other and formed an instant love for each other.

I often found myself staring at Sami and wishing I could read her mind. Sitting in a hospital room with a birth mother and her family is an uncomfortable situation for any adoptive parent. But I knew my discomfort would be temporary. I knew if all went well the next day, Sami would be discharged, and I would be able to step fully into my role as mother.

The sky turned dark, and people began to yawn, so around nine o'clock, we felt it was time for us to leave. Everyone was ready for some much-needed sleep.

I didn't want to leave my son in that room. I wanted to be with him during his first night of life. I wanted to cuddle him and smell him, wrap his tiny fingers around mine. I wanted to sing him soft lullabies. When he would wake up, hungry and afraid in this new world, I wanted to be the one to comfort him. I wanted the sound of my heartbeat and the smell of my skin to be the very things to ease the cries and soften the fears. But I looked at Sami holding him and knew she wanted all those things as well. And this was the only night she would have them.

Josh seemed to sense my reticence, the physical pain I felt in my heart. He grabbed my hand and held on tight as we made our way down the elevator, through the sliding glass doors, and into the cold night air.

I woke up early after a restless night. I didn't mind the lack of sleep, for every minute I was awake I had been thinking about August, and when I did drift off, he met me in my dreams.

I sat up in the hotel bed at the first sign of light. Beyond the window, another beautiful day began to unfold. Yet as the sun began to rise and the world stretched out to receive its warmth, a strange fog consumed me. It wasn't thick enough to block out the sun, just thick enough to make me aware of its gloom. I didn't try to ignore it, nor did I try to pray it away. It was an appropriate fog, and wise in its timing.

This was the day on which birth mom, sister, aunts, and grandma would say good-bye to the baby they loved. So while I could hardly stand being away from my son for one more second, I embraced this fog and let it wrap itself around me, because, really, what else was I to do?

Josh and I spent the morning in our hotel room waiting for Lucy to let us know it was okay to come back to the hospital. While Josh went to get us Americanos with an extra shot of espresso, I called my parents and sisters to give them an update. I sent out mass text messages to the army of friends who had supported us and prayed us to this point.

The minutes on the clock passed slowly, and then around ten o'clock, my phone finally dinged with a message from Lucy, letting us know it was okay to come. She also told us the doctor had expressed concern that August was a little jaundiced, so a decision had been made to give him phototherapy. He would need to stay at the hospital for at least one more night.

We were so disappointed to learn this new bit of information. We had let all our family and friends know we would be coming home that day. On our way to the hospital, I called my mom.

"We won't be coming home today after all."

"What happened? Is everything okay?"

"Yes, everything is fine. He has some jaundice, so the doctors want to give him a day of light therapy. Are you and Dad okay with the girls for another night?"

"Of course!"

"I wish you guys could be here with us." I was missing my girls and wanted them to meet their brother.

"Heather, we're doing great. Don't worry about us. Just do what you need to do and know that your girls are being taken care of."

"Thanks, Mom." Tears welled in my eyes. My lack of sleep and the emotional weight of the situation had finally made its way to the forefront of my mind. "I have to go. I'll keep you posted, though. Thank you for loving my girls. Give them a huge kiss from me."

"Of course, sweetheart. We are praying for all of you. I love you."

"I love you too." I hung up the phone just as Josh parked the car in the hospital parking lot.

As we went up to August's room, the lingering fog that had

wrapped itself around me that morning thickened. Yesterday had been full of celebration, laughter, and joy as we passed August around, taking turns holding him, feeding him, and changing his diaper. But today would be different.

When we opened the door of the hospital room, we were met by an obnoxious blue glow. August lay in his hospital bassinet under a giant blue light in nothing but a diaper. A mask covered his eyes. We politely greeted the aunties, grandma, Joy, and Sami, and then I noticed it: this blue light was laying claim to everyone in the room, as though its glow had the power to expose the many thoughts and emotions bouncing off the walls. We all stared at the baby under the light that illuminated all of our faces and revealed the weight of grief. By the end of the day, Sami would be discharged. Once again, I was slapped with the truth that my gain would be another's loss.

We spent much of the day just looking at the precious masked baby. I wanted to hold him. My arms craved the six-pound eleven-ounce weight of his body. My lips craved the roundness of his cheeks. But that light owned him for most of the time. Once every two hours he could come out to eat and get a fresh diaper. We all watched the clock, and as soon as the two hours were up, Sami or one of her sisters would turn off the light, take off the mask, and scoop him up.

I so badly wanted to be the one to rescue him from the ugly lights, but it was not my turn yet. By day's end, I would be the only mother in the room. For every ounce Sami fed him, I would get to feed him a thousand more. For every diaper she changed, I would get to change a thousand more. For every word of love she whispered in his ears, I would get to whisper a thousand more. So I sat in the discomfort of a mother who could do nothing more than observe her child. God gently reminded me that Sami would be an observing mother for the rest of her life. I could do it for that one day.

Around noon, I got word that a social worker from the adoption agency was on her way to the hospital. Sami would sign her relinquishment of rights today, but legally this couldn't happen until she was discharged from the hospital.

As soon as the social worker walked into the blue-tinted room, I felt two simultaneous urges. I wanted to run out and avoid the pain those relinquishment papers would cause, and I wanted to jump in front of Sami, this new person whom I felt deep love for, and protect her from the unspeakable and inevitable pain of being severed from her child. Instead, I sat there waiting for someone to tell me what to do.

"Do you mind if I have some time alone with Sami?" She looked at each face in the room, gently asking us to leave.

"Of course not," Josh said.

"How about lunch?" I offered. "Sami, can we bring you anything?"

"No, I'm good. Thank you." There was sorrow in her voice.

"We'll join you," Sami's sister Brittany said.

Sami looked at her sister Lucy. "Will you stay with me?"

"Of course."

Josh, Brittany, Tandy, Joy, and I all headed to the hospital cafeteria.

Years ago, if I had found myself leaving my son and his birth mother behind so she could hold him in one hand and sign away her rights to him with the other—or change her mind and decide not to—I would have been a terrified wreck. I would have flailed around looking for something, anything, I could control. And I would have come up empty and exhausted. Yes, I felt extremely uncomfortable in that moment, and yes, I still longed for control over the situation, but more than that, I felt God's peace. I heard him whisper, "Look at all I've done so far. Heather, I've got this."

I knew it to be true. I'd lived in that truth. I couldn't imagine the pain I would feel if Sami refused to sign. I couldn't think of the agony that would grip me if I wasn't allowed to become August's mother. But I also knew that God's goodness is good no matter what.

When we returned from lunch, the social worker was waiting for us in the lobby. Josh and I sat down with her, and she let us know that Sami had signed the necessary papers. As she told us, I smiled, but the fog that had greeted me earlier that morning and lingered throughout the day suddenly felt thicker than ever. To sit in the lobby rejoicing while Sami mourned in her hospital room did not seem appropriate. This day was messy and complicated. While part of me wanted to make everything feel good, I knew the best and most appropriate thing to do was sit in the mess and let all the emotions unfold. We needed to feel it all: the good, the difficult, the joy, the pain. So when I signed my name on the adoption papers that day, claiming August as my own, I let the reality of adoption, of my joy being another's sadness, rest on me.

Signing the papers made Josh and me August's legal guardians. Now we had the rights to care for August in the hospital. For a nominal fee we would be allowed to stay with August in our own hospital room. We also found out that Sami's final discharge papers were complete and that she, along with her family, would be leaving soon.

Back in August's blue room, we all waited for the two-hour mark when he could come out from under the light to be fed and have his diaper changed. Sami's bags were packed and waiting by the door. At the appointed time, Sami went over to her sweet baby boy, clicked off the blue light, and gently picked him up.

She removed the mask and cradled him in her arms as she softly ran the back of her hand across his fresh cheeks. With tears streaming from her eyes, she whispered, "I love you" into his ear. Time stood still, and everyone in the room wept with her and poured out our love on this perfect baby boy. Lucy handed her a fresh bottle, and we all watched as she sat on the bed to feed him one last time.

By the time he finished his bottle, it was almost time for him to go back under the blue light. Sami handed him to Lucy, and for the next few minutes, he was passed around the room as aunties, grandma, and sister said good-bye. Then Sami held him close one more time, closing her eyes and pressing her face against his head. After one more "I love you," he was back under the obnoxious blue light.

Everyone gave Josh a quick and teary hug, and he stayed with August as I walked out with them.

No one said a word. We did what had to be done and put one foot in front of the other as we headed to the elevator. One foot in front of the other into the elevator, tear-filled eyes glued to the floor. The door opened, and we put one foot in front of the other out of the hospital and into the cool evening air and all the way to their car.

Saying good-bye to Sami and her family was brutal. The loss they were experiencing weighed on me in a way I didn't expect. I embraced her sisters and mom.

"Thank you for everything! For the gifts and the love. Thank you!" I said through tears.

"Take good care of him. We know you will," Lucy said as she wept on my shoulder.

"I will. I promise I will."

I gave Joy a long, tight hug, "You can see your brother any time you want. You just have your mommy call me, okay?"

She smiled and hugged me back, her youth offering her some protection from the gravity of the moment.

Then I made my way toward Sami. We wrapped our arms around each other and sobbed. As I drenched her shoulder with my tears, I thought about how less than forty-eight hours ago, she had August in her womb, where she loved him and cared for him with all that she was. Now her womb and her arms were empty.

"I'm so sorry this is so hard," I whispered. "I am so proud of you, Sami. I have never seen someone do such a selfless thing."

"I love him so much, Heather."

"I know you do."

"Promise me you'll take good care of him." Her words came out broken and slurred between the sobs.

"I promise, Sami. The best care possible."

We broke our embrace, and she got into the front seat of the car. I stood there in the cold parking garage and watched them drive away.

the Lucky Few

We had the joy of bringing August home only forty-eight hours after he was born. This was an unexpected delight. All too often, babies with Down syndrome need some kind of immediate medical attention. When the doctors said that August could go home just two days after he took his first breath of life in this world, I thanked God for his favor.

I sat next to my son as we drove the two and a half hours home. I could hardly wait to see my girls and watch them meet their new little brother. Though I had only been gone for two days, they were life-altering days, and I was missing my girls something fierce.

We pulled up to signs littering our lawn and plastered across the door, welcoming our son home. My heart swelled at the love that friends and family continued to pour out on us.

Josh parked in the driveway, and I unbuckled August's car seat harness and scooped up all seven pounds of him. Before we opened the door to go inside, Josh put his arm around my shoulder, as he had done two times before in this exact location, and we both stared at the baby in my arms.

"He's here. He's perfect," Josh said.

"I know. I'm blown away by God's goodness."

"We have three kids!" Josh laughed.

"Welcome to Crazyville!" I laughed along with him as we opened the door and stepped inside.

The second the door opened, we were greeted by the cheers and squeals of two excited big sisters. They ran into Josh's arms. He gathered them up, one big sister on each hip, and I leaned over to give each of them a kiss and introduce them to their new baby brother.

"Can I hold him?" Truly asked.

"Hold him?" Macyn repeated.

"Of course, girls. Let's go wash your hands first. You always have to wash your hands before touching your baby brother, okay?" We were in the middle of cold and flu season. Once again, hand washing in the Avis household became as important as breathing.

Josh walked with the girls to the bathroom. I stepped into the living room, where both my parents and Josh's parents stood, all four of them anxious to meet their new grandson, all four crying happy tears.

"Oh, Heather," my mother-in-law, Jay, said as she came over and put her arm around me and gave me a big squeeze. "He's perfect!"

"He really is," my father-in-law, Steve, agreed as he stared at his new grandson.

"Wanna hold him?" I asked.

"Yes!" they blurted out simultaneously.

We spent the next few hours passing August around while he slept through all the excitement. I sat on the couch with my mom and Jay and recalled the events of the past two days. As August went from grandparent to grandparent, big sister Macyn never left his side.

That first night home, after the grandparents said their good-byes and the big sisters were tucked into their beds, Josh and I sat on our bed with August lying between us. We didn't talk; we just stared at the tiny sleeping human. Josh got up to brush his teeth, and I lay down next to August, settling into the fluffy white down comforter, my nose touching his. I closed my eyes and breathed deeply. As I felt his breath on my lips and smelled his fresh, sweet skin, I was overcome by awe and wonder. I was now the mother of three children. I had no control over how these children made their way into the world. Josh and I could never have contributed to the creation of these children with our blood and DNA. I could have searched the world for three lifetimes and never been able to find these three children, my children, on my own.

I breathed in the miracle of my son and thought about the miracle of the two little girls asleep in the next room. I had so much love for all three of them. Oh, the love! When I was desperate to be a mother and unable to make it happen on my own, I had no idea this kind of love would consume every part of my being. It was unexplainable.

I always say you can't know what you don't know, and if I had never adopted a newborn baby, I would never have known what I was missing during that wonderful phase. Thanks to Jesus, I got to experience what I like to call newborn-baby bliss.

I know a lot of moms who would say that the first few months with their newborn baby were anything but blissful, but our situation was unique. I got to bring home an angel baby. I mean *angel baby*. He was a good sleeper and a good eater. He was easygoing and rarely cried, and when he did, he responded to the remedy quickly. And I felt great. Of course, I was tired from the middle-of-the-night feedings, but my body had not just experienced the travail of giving birth.

August and I also were able to experience the bonding that can more easily take place with a newborn. Of course, there's something to be said for the nine months in utero where he bonded with his birth mother. But unlike my girls, who spent the first months of their lives bonding with a different mother, I was the only mother August knew. So our bond was strong.

Life with three kids under five years old, two of whom had Down syndrome, was no walk in the park. Our lives resembled some kind of a circus. But I found myself giddy about being able to wrap my baby on my chest and take a daughter's hand in each of mine and jump through the fiery hoops or occasionally stick my head in the lion's mouth.

It was wild and crazy, but our family life was soaked in God's grace.

Within weeks of August's birth, I found myself in the same waiting room I had been in with Macyn five years earlier. We were there for the same reason—waiting to meet with a cardiologist to discuss the best way to prepare for August's unavoidable open-heart surgery.

Behind the desk were the same people signing August in, and behind the doors the same nurses and doctors stood ready to measure, weigh, and prescribe. They all recognized me, and some even knew me by name. But I was not the same woman. As I waited there with August wrapped up against my chest, sound asleep, I felt our hearts beating side by side. His heart was weak, but mine was stronger than it had ever been.

Five years ago, I held on to Macyn with both hands. Our hearts were beating side by side, but both were weak and sick. Both were in need of healing. As I walked through the valley of the shadow of death with Macyn during her surgery, and really during the first few years of her life, I was too immersed in her healing to be able to recognize the healing taking place in me.

Now as I waited with August, I did so as a mother who was a child as well. I knew I could not take one step as a parent without first taking the hand of my heavenly Father.

We scheduled August's open-heart surgery for the end of April. On that day in 2014, we showed up at the same hospital, made our way through the same double doors, and waited in the same waiting area. The doors and walls of this familiar place reminded us of God's good, good grace.

Sending a child into open-heart surgery is never an easy task. But I knew I would be comforted when I rested fully in God. When Josh and I began our journey into parenthood, I never would have chosen a children's hospital as a significant character in our story, yet somehow she had worked her way into the fabric of our lives.

Within her walls, I met God in the most intimate ways. Eventually, every time I entered, I could do so with hope and joy rather than fear. And isn't that just like our God—to take the very things in life we should be terrified of and to cover them with his goodness and beauty?

Josh, August, and I had been in the pre-op room for about an hour when a nurse came and tapped me on the shoulder.

"Sorry to interrupt, but there is a woman named Sami in the hallway. She said you're expecting her?" The nurse seemed confused.

"Oh yes, she's our son's birth mother." I said it as though having our adopted child's birth mother at his open-heart surgery was to be expected. "Can she come in?" Sami had contacted me a few weeks before Augie's surgery, asking if she could come. Josh and I both felt comfortable with her being there.

The nurse, looking even more perplexed, simply nodded and let Sami in.

"How's he doing?" Sami carried a purse and a stuffed bear with a Band-Aid sewn over its heart. She walked toward August, who was in my arms. I gave her a side hug with my free hand.

"He's so great. Hasn't had anything to eat or drink since dinner last night, and he hasn't complained at all." I looked at the baby cradled in my arm. "Here, why don't you hold him?"

Sami set the purse and bear on the hospital bed. "Hey, buddy." She lifted him over her shoulder and gave him a squeeze.

At that exact moment, our son's heart surgeon came over to give August one last look. He looked at me, then at Sami holding my baby, and then back at me.

I tried to answer his surprised expression. "This is Sami, August's birth mother."

"Oh." A common response to a unique situation. No one is ever sure quite what to say. He pulled out his stethoscope and placed it on August's chest. We all stood there quietly. "Okay, he's good." Then he looked at the nurse. "We're ready."

"Wait." They may have been ready, but I was not. "I'm going to need a one-minute warning."

The nurse gave me a sweet smile. "One minute."

Sami gave August a kiss on the forehead and handed him back to me. Josh came over and took him from my arms. "I love you so much, buddy. You are strong and brave." He kissed August's soft cheeks.

"I need him back." I reached for my son, and Josh placed him in my arms once more. I hugged him and kissed him.

"Okay, it's time." The nurse held out her arms.

"You'll make sure he's all right?" I begged through tears.

"I promise I will not leave his side." I handed the nurse my son, and we watched her walk away, his tiny head bouncing gently.

The three of us made our way to the waiting area, where we were greeted by our social worker and friends holding extra-large lattes and vanilla-bean scones. We sat in a corner of the waiting area, moving chairs around, throwing down our purses and bags, claiming our space for the next five or six hours.

Conversation went from surgery to babies to the weather to favorite travel destinations. A few hours later, Josh grabbed my hand.

"You wanna go for a walk?"

"I would love some fresh air." I said to our waiting-room crew, "We'll be back soon."

We stepped outside to a cloudy and slightly chilly spring day. "I had to get out of there," Josh said, putting his arm around my shoulder. "I'm not in the mood for small talk right now."

"Neither am I." I wrapped my arm around his waist, and we began to walk the perimeter of the hospital.

"Do you feel different this time around?" Josh asked.

"Yes! Like a completely different person."

"Me too."

"It sounds crazy to say so, but I just feel like open-heart surgery isn't that big of a deal." I looked up at my husband. "*Is* that crazy?"

"I feel the same way." Josh's arm slipped from my shoulder, and his fingers interlocked with mine. "We've seen God do so much, and, really, open-heart surgery isn't that big of a deal."

"Yeah, but could you ever imagine we'd be saying this?" I stopped and turned toward Josh. "I mean, look at us. We're sitting in a waiting room with our son's birth mother, waiting for him to come out of open-heart surgery, and we're cool as cucumbers."

"Yeah, it's crazy."

"I wish my twenty-four-year-old self could see this and know how good it would all turn out."

"Or maybe understand that just because circumstances are hard, it doesn't mean they're bad."

"Yeah." I let out a small sigh. "I wish I knew God then like I do now."

"Me too. But I don't think it would have been possible if not for saying yes to Macyn and every other step that led us to this place." As soon as Josh finished his thought, the pager we had been given to keep us updated on Augie's surgery went off.

I jumped. "It says they're closing him up."

"Whoa! That was fast. Let's go."

August's surgery went great. After a few days in the hospital, his doctors sent him home. A week later, at the follow-up appointment, his surgeon took him off two of the three medications he had been on. A couple of weeks after that, we were back into the swing of our full and crazy life.

The day-to-day activities and needs that accompany three small children and their special needs is no joke. Our day-to-day routines are anything but normal. The staring and pointing we get when we walk through the Target parking lot or step foot into a restaurant have become a part of *our* normal. We've chosen to make our normal *great* by meeting the stares with sweet smiles, and the rude or ignorant comments with a little sass.

We rarely take all three kids to the grocery store at the same time if we can avoid it. But from time to time, we'll be near a Trader Joe's, and amnesia will sink in. We'll forget about the last time we had all three children in the tiny market, and we'll look at each other with grand confidence and step into the store like fools.

We place August's car seat on the handlebar/kid seat of the cart, Augie inside, sleeping like an angel. That's all the time it takes for Macyn and Truly to break away. They've spotted the samples booth at the back of the store.

"Truly, Macyn, stop!" I yell. Truly obeys, but Macyn keeps going.

"Macyn!" Truly yells after her.

I leave Josh with August and pass up Truly, saying, "I'll get her, Tru." I catch Macy just in time to grab her before she crashes into an unsuspecting elderly woman walking with a walker.

"Oh my!" the woman exclaims.

"I'm so sorry," I say to her, and then I kneel down next to Macyn. "Macy, you have to stay with Mama in the store. You cannot run away."

"Okay."

"Well, hello," the kind elderly woman says to Macyn.

"Hello." Macy gives a sweet wave and a smile.

The woman leans toward me. "She has the Downs, huh?"

I cringe inside at the crass terminology and try to be gentle in my correction. "She *does* have Down syndrome."

Josh arrives. "Hey, there you are." He pushes the cart next to our little party by the Trader Joe's samples booth. The woman glances at Augie, now awake, in his car seat.

"Oh my. You have two of them."

I glance at Josh, and we give each other a look.

"We have three kids, in fact." Josh smiles and picks up Truly, whose mouth is full of coffee cake samples.

The sweet elderly woman leans in again and says conspiratorially, "You know, they'll be with you forever." She raises her eyebrows.

I give her a wink. "Gosh, I hope so."

"Mommy! Sample!" Macyn pulls on my hand.

"You take care," Josh says as we walk away. Then he looks at me. "Let's be quick."

I hold Truly's hand and place Macyn in the back of the cart. Josh pushes, and we make our way up and down the aisles, filling the remainder of the cart with some of our essentials.

By the time we reach the checkout counter, August has begun to fuss.

"Babe, hand me the diaper bag?" I let go of Truly's hand and pull out a bottle and some formula.

"Hang in there, buddy," Josh says over and over to our crying baby.

Macyn begins to shovel our items out of the cart, throwing them toward the cashier.

"Macyn, stop." I grab the eggs with one hand, just in time, while shaking the formula bottle with the other.

"So sorry." I smile apologetically at the man behind the register.

"Where's Truly?" Josh asks as he grabs the bottle from me and places it in our now screaming baby's mouth.

The cashier points to a curly-haired girl with boxes of cookies in her hands.

"Tru!" I run toward her and begin stacking the boxes back on the shelf as neatly as I can. "You have to stay with Mommy and Daddy."

The man looks at me as I walk back toward our cart. "You guys have your hands full."

I give him a pathetic grin, understanding this statement is never a compliment. Josh says, "Oh man, you're telling me! We just found out we're pregnant with twins."

The man looks at us in shock. I give a stoic and confirming nod.

Whenever we take our children out in public, we're guaranteed to get stares, pointing fingers, and lots and lots of double takes.

Our family makeup is unique. If I were to see my family out in public, I'd be curious and probably stare a bit. So rather than be easily offended or pretend to be normal, we try to face it with openness, grace, and a little humor. We chose to adopt two kids with Down syndrome and one kid of a race different from ours. We *have* to be okay with people being surprised by that. We're proud of our family, and we want others to feel that way too.

Josh and I have made a conscious decision to be open with our children, as well as with the world, about how our family came to be. People often want to know when we told our kids they were adopted, and our answer is they have always known. Adoption is a part of who they are, so it has never been a secret. Rather, we celebrate it and thank God for it, because without adoption, our family would not exist.

As a mixed-race, mixed-ability, adoptive family (wow, say that ten times fast), we've learned we must be intentional in the way we live our lives and raise our kids. Our relationships with birth parents are one example of this. Josh and I believe it is important for our adopted kids to know where they came from, as much as is beneficial for them. Our situation is unique in that two of our kids come from birth families we are able to have a relationship with. It would have been so much easier for us to have minimal contact with our children's birth families. It's difficult enough making quality time happen with our extended family. The effort it takes to maintain intimate and healthy relationships with two more whole families is immense.

In contrast, we know little about Truly's birth family, and pieces of what we do know could, in fact, harm her. We have found we need to be careful in how we address Truly's need for connection to where she came from. When she asked about her birth mother for the first time, we were age-appropriately honest, and this means leaving out some of the facts, at least for now, to protect our daughter.

Another area in which we work hard is that of race awareness. Both Josh and I grew up in a small, predominantly white mountain town. My predominantly white high school pointed me toward a predominantly white college, and we ended up living the first half of our marriage in a predominantly white town. When we began our adoption journey, I knew it was likely we would receive a child who was not white. When Macyn came home, although her skin color matched my own, I made sure she had dolls of every skin tone and books reflecting racial diversity.

When we got the call about a "Guatemalan baby" and soon learned she was both Guatemalan and African American, we made some drastic changes to our life habits. After Truly had been with us for only a few months, we started driving more than an hour each way to attend a church with children, men, and women who looked like her. After about a year of this, we decided to move from our comfortable, mostly white community to a much more racially diverse neighborhood. We needed to make sure there would be women in Truly's life who look like her, because the day will come when she says to me, "Mom, you just don't get it." I want to be able to say to her, "Honey, you're right; go talk to Auntie Tiana about that."

It's important to Josh and me that our children grow up with a strong identity. We believe our children will forever adore the people who gave them life, so we want them to be able to do so out in the open, where we can join them in the adoration, thus doing away with any of the shame waiting to pounce. We also hope to one day gather more information about Truly's birth mother so she can hold those missing pieces with both of her hands. But in the meantime, as she sees us celebrate her siblings' birth families, we can openly talk about her birth mother, and she can ask me questions without any guilt or shame because she sees how much love I have for birth parents.

I cannot begin to count the hours I have spent in doctor's offices and hospital waiting rooms and at physical therapy, occupational therapy, oral-motor therapy, and speech therapy appointments. Josh and I strongly believe we are responsible to provide Macyn and August with all the services they need to live with Down syndrome at their fullest potential. This is something we committed to when we decided to adopt them. Since Macyn came home to be ours, we've had anywhere from two to eight hours of therapy a week. This doesn't include the time on the phone to secure these appointments, nor does it include the hours in the car driving to and from these appointments.

We live in a society that puts pressure on all of us to acquire and maintain some sort of acceptability. Whether my children with Down syndrome should have to strive to be "acceptable" in anyone's eyes is not the point here. (I'll save that topic for my next book.) The fact is, my children who have Down syndrome have to work hard at what comes naturally to you, me, and our typical kids. I believe providing them with therapy gives them the best chance to succeed at these tasks.

Being intentional is often uncomfortable. But this is something we signed up for. For every yes that each of my children represent, there is an equally important no to our comfort. And having said those three yeses, we feel so lucky. Lucky, because every time we find ourselves waist-deep in discomfort, we also find ourselves leaning on God, experiencing his comfort and peace.

I've been up since three forty-five this morning. It's not quite eight at night now, but I'm ready to find my way into my comfy pj's and nestle under my flannel sheets. It's almost Christmas. We woke up before the sun to get a head start on the 484 miles of road that leads to a town called Chico, where we will be with my husband's family to celebrate the birth of Jesus and bask in the wonder of all things Christmas. As I write this, I am sitting in a cozy living room, looking at the brightly lit Christmas tree covered in an array of shiny ornaments. I'm so very tired.

I have decided my three scrumptious children are to blame for my fatigue. I'm pretty sure I've been tired for the past seven years. Writing this book has been a gift, an opportunity to reflect on those years that marked the birth of our family. As I do so, I can see why I am exhausted. Not once before having children did I imagine how much of myself would be required when my three munchkins entered my life.

As I write this, Macyn, Truly, and August are sound asleep downstairs. (Actually, there is a good chance Truly is wide-awake, trying to think of another excuse to get out of bed.) As they peacefully dream in their cozy beds, I can feel my heart being pulled toward theirs, beating in tandem.

Tonight, like every night, before I head to bed, I will check on each one of them, pulling their covers up to their chins and kissing each of those button noses, praying a prayer of thanksgiving, protection, and grace over each of their sleeping bodies. I will crawl into my bed knowing that one, two, or all three of them will be up before the sun comes up. I expect that tomorrow I will prepare three meals, referee disagreements, point out all the messes they made and now should clean up, participate in and DJ dance parties, wipe bottoms, spot August as he climbs up and down the stairs at least a hundred times, talk Macyn through the dozens of situations she finds too difficult, repeat myself because no one seems to listen, color with Truly, dance some more, jump on the trampoline, hand out ice packs because someone is going to fall or bonk their head, implement therapy, and schedule some kind of doctor's appointment. If I'm lucky, I'll take a shower.

This is the life of a mother. It is the life of any mother of a child or children who have special needs. But somehow, at the end of every long and full day, I find that though I am tired, I am not worn-out. I am tired but not spent. I am tired but always full, because my joy is so much bigger than my exhaustion. There is always so much joy.

About two years ago, I had just finished tucking the kids in bed. I poured myself a glass of wine, grabbed my phone, planted myself on my couch, and started scrolling through our Instagram account, @macymakesmyday. I stumbled upon a comment thread that stopped me in my tracks.

"@annyhoang you should follow this account."

She replied, "I already do! This family is a huge reason we're adopting Ruthie."

Wait, what does this mean? I wondered, and I began to click on links to try to find out what exactly this person meant. I finally found a way to leave @annyhoang a message.

Hi, my name is Heather and I read a comment you posted on our Instagram account @macymakesmyday. You said

something about adopting a little girl named Ruthie.
I wonder if you could tell me more.

The woman, Ann, responded right away.

Hi, Heather. So great hearing from you. My husband and
I are actually in China right now, picking up our adopted
daughter. Her name is Ruthie, she's five years old, and
she has Down syndrome. You and your family were our
inspiration for adopting a child with Down syndrome.

I held my phone in my hands and read and reread her message. And I cried. I couldn't even believe it. I was floored to know our little story unfolding in our neck of the woods was reaching far beyond us and grabbing hold of the life of another little girl who has Down syndrome—a little girl who had been waiting in an orphanage in China for a family to call her own.

Eight years ago, God shined a light into my wilderness, and Josh and I stepped off our path of easy, normal, and nice to go after it. He took our muddied clothes, tired souls, and broken hearts, and from our humble offerings created a crazy masterpiece. He took our meager yes and used it to stir up hearts and change lives.

There is absolutely no way to know the ripple effect we create when we say yes to God's seemingly terrifying invitation. Ann's story is just one of dozens I've been told by soon-to-be moms and dads who are in the process of adopting a child with Down syndrome and were encouraged by what they've seen in our family. Numerous women have contacted me to say that Macyn and August have given them hope for their baby newly diagnosed with Down syndrome.

I don't share this to say, "Hey, look at what we've done over here with our lives." The truth is, I'm average at best. But I serve a grand God, and I've been lucky enough to answer when he calls. He does the rest.

When we adopted Macyn, we had no intention of doing so as a way to be encouraging to others. As we stepped toward her and Truly and August, we had no one on our minds but our little family unit and our God. As we threw our yes pebble in the stagnant and murky waters of our lives, we did not think about the ripples the pebble would create.

I believe that at some point in our lives each of us has the opportunity to leave our comfortable path and head into the wilderness. Each of us will at some point hold a "yes pebble" in our hands. My hope and prayer for all of us is that we will be willing to toss those pebbles into the murky waters and get our fancy shoes dirty in the mud. My hope is that as we say yes, the ripples of our decisions will begin to form wonderful waves. Waves, my friends, cannot be ignored.

I wake up every day excited and a tiny bit terrified as I look forward to hearing God's call. Upon first glance at my rambunctious children, the ones jumping on my bed, ready for the day before the sun has come up, I'm reminded of just how lucky I am to be in this place and in this time. I think about how lucky all of us are when we finally allow God to gently push us toward the places where he's waiting to be discovered. Not a whole lot of us choose to leave that path of easy, normal, and nice, the one covered in rose petals and lined with solar-powered lamps. But for those of us who do, we really and truly are the lucky few.

Acknowledgments

I have crossed paths with many people who have been an enormous encouragement and whose expertise, love, and prayers have helped bring this book to fruition. Honestly? I can hardly believe I get to write down this epic list:

Lisa Gungor, August's future mother-in-law (there, I've said it; it's official)—thanks for inviting me to the Holy Land, for without that invitation, there's a good chance this book would not exist.

Emily Vogeltanz, Ally Falon, Betsy Miller, Lisa Gungor, Shauna Niequist, Tamara Wytsma, and Vickie Reddy—who knew that all those hours on a bus in the Holy Land could knit such sweet friendships? Thank you for being an encouragement in my life.

Rachel Hollis—for your friendship and expertise, and for pouring me a glass of wine at just the right moments. I love you, girl!

Don and Betsy Miller—for your generosity, humble hearts, and expert advice.

Ann Voskamp and Shauna Niequist—thank you for short notes sent to important people. Pretty sure this book is on bookshelves because of those.

My agent, Lisa Jackson—friend, you saw this book before I ever imagined it could be. Thank you for your constant belief in me, your adoration for my family, and your desire to see this story God has given me in the pages of a book.

My editor Erin Healy—for hearing my voice and making it sing. You have taught me so much. Thank you.

Carolyn McCready and all the folks at Zondervan—thank you for seeing the potential in me, for seeing God's goodness in this story, and for working so hard to help me share it with the masses.

Courtney and Tuna (@tunameltsmyheart)—remember that time you told me I should start an Instagram account? Good idea!

The @macymakesmyday community—you bless my socks off daily with your kindness, love, and support. Let's continue to join our voices as we Shout Their Worth.

My friends in the Down syndrome community—what an honor and a privilege it is to know you, to learn from you, and to do life alongside you (even if for some, it's only through social media)! Our hearts and lives are bound by an extra chromosome, which is a gift we do not take lightly.

My children's birth families—this is my story because of you. Thank you for your loving sacrifice.

Katie and Danny, Joy and Kyle, Brandon and Michelle, Jen and Rey, Christine and Dave—you have been my loudest and most consistent cheerleaders with every word I've written in this book. God brought you into my life to do life with at the exact moment I would need you most. Thank you for your never-ending support, love, and prayers. Let's continue to always toast the small things and the big. I love you all.

My village—Lindsey, Cynthia, Erika, Kelly, and Laura—your friendship has filled my cup time and time again. Let's do life together forever, yeah?

Jay and Steve, my mother-in-love and father-in-love—for your never-ending positivity, and for always being available to help with the kids. I love you so very much!

My parents—Josh, the kids, and I would be nothing without your constant support and saturating love. Thank you for joining us as we grip the life God has called us to. I cannot love you more.

My sisters and best friends, Hana and Harmony—you are my pillars. Thank you for standing strong when my strength gave out and for always believing in this crazy plan that God had for my life.

My husband, Josh—babe, look at the photo on the cover of this book! Can you even believe this is where we've landed? Thank you for adventuring with me. There is not another person on this earth I would have wanted to walk down this path with. Yours is the only hand I wanted to hold as we walked the miles to get us to this place. Can't wait to see what God has in store for us as we walk one million more. You have my heart!

And finally and forever, Jesus—thank you, Jesus, for rocking my world. Thank you for equipping me to say yes to your best plan for my life, even though it seemed so dang scary at first. Your goodness knows no bounds.

Recommended Resources

My greatest resources have always been the people whose paths cross mine. I listen to their stories and ask questions about their experiences. I also highly recommend a good ol' Google search for adoption networks in your area. The following websites are ones I frequent:

Club 21, clubtwentyone.org—a learning and resource center for individuals with Down syndrome

National Down Syndrome Society, ndss.org—an advocacy group promoting the value, acceptance, and inclusion of individuals with Down syndrome

National Down Syndrome Adoption Network, ndsan.org—a free service providing information and support to families who are making adoption plans or seeking to adopt a child with Down syndrome

Rage Against the Minivan, rageagainsttheminivan.com—insights into transracial adoption and parenting, with links to many helpful resources for adoptive families

About the Author

Heather Avis is wife to her handsome and hardworking man, Josh, and mother to the adorable Macyn, Truly, and August. After working as an education specialist, she found herself as a full-time stay-at-home mom when she and her husband adopted their first daughter, Macyn, in 2008. Shortly thereafter, in 2011, they adopted their second daughter, Truly. And in 2013, their son, August, was born and came home to be theirs. Heather currently resides in Southern California, where between oatmeal making, diaper changing, and dance parties she is using her hit Instagram account @macymakesmyday to share the awesomeness of all things Down syndrome and adoption. She cares fiercely for the underdog and believes God's goodness and beauty are found in the most unexpected places.